TYPE, IMAGE, MESSAGE

ROCKPORT

GLOUCESTER MASSACHUSETTS

ROCKPORT

PUBLISHERS

TYPE, IMAGE, MESSAGE

A GRAPHIC DESIGN LAYOUT WORKSHOP

NANCY SKOLOS

THOMAS WEDELL

First published in the United States of America by Rockport Publishers, a member of Quayside Publishing Group

33 Commercial Street

Gloucester, Massachusetts 01930-5089

Telephone: (978) 282-9590

Fax: (978) 283-2742

www.rockpub.com

Library of Congress Cataloging-in-Publication Data

Skolos, Nancy.

Type, image, message : a graphic design layout workshop/ Nancy Skolos, Thomas Wedell.

p.   cm.

Includes index.

ISBN 1-59253-189-X (hardcover)

1. Commercial art—History—21st century. 2. Graphic arts—History—21st century. 3. Communication in design. 4. Graphic design (Typography) I. Wedell, Thomas. II. Title.

NC998.4S56 2006

741.609'0511—dc22   2005032021
                                     CIP

ISBN 1-59253-189-X

Printed in China

PROJECT
Untitled #30
(fine art photography)
PHOTOGRAPHER
Matt Siber
Chicago, USA

It has often been said that a picture is worth a thousand words.
More recently in a lecture at the Rhode Island School of Design, multimedia designer
Mikon van Gastel offered, "One perfectly chosen word is worth thirty minutes of footage."
Value judgments aside, one thing is clear: graphic designers are both blessed and cursed for working with
two very distinct modes of communication, the word and the image.

As in any successful partnership, type and image work best when they complement each other—when
they finish each other's sentences. For graphic designers, a photograph isn't finished with a click of
the shutter. That is just the beginning of the creative process, as an image becomes a part of a
piece of graphic design. In fact, the image must be "incomplete" so there is something left for
the type to do.

In the conceptual phase of a project, designers often begin working with type and image
intuitively, in a mind space where the two are more like substances than entities. We
experience them, imagine them, see them in our sleep, and consider them simultaneously.
They never operate outside of a context and their meaning is never fully realized until they
are put into play. Often they are assigned a "format" within which to interact. They can be
visualized with common textures, shapes, and colors, and unified with light or shadow,
but even in the realm of our greatest imagination, they remain uniquely discernible
as type or image.

The viewer depends on type and image to give form and meaning to many
messages and ideas. Both contain room for interpretation by the audience and
extend the role of the graphic designer from form giver to mediator and guide.
Through form, designers construct and create an organized system for content,
emphasizing some concepts and de-emphasizing others, providing ways into,
around, and out of each work.

While much has been written about typography and photography,
surprisingly little has been written about how the two work together.
Many times while in the final throes of completing a project that
employs both type and image, designers will confess, "I'm just no good
with type." The reality is that nobody is naturally good at combining
type and image. Even though words and images are familiar ways of
expressing human experience, the two forms of communication
are inherently difficult to reconcile. This book is intended
to begin to fill that gap. We call it a "graphic design layout
workshop" because it originates from a place of *making* as
much as *analyzing*. Pioneering, innovative graphic designers
and photographers from around the world have contributed
their extraordinary designs to this endeavor, and it is their
inspiration within these pages that serves as the backbone
of this discussion and possible reconciliation.

FORM

INTRODUCTION

Space and Point(s) of Entry:

"Reading" a photograph is very different from reading a text.
For example, in Western culture, a conventional hierarchy is well
established, dictating a left-to-right, top-to-bottom approach.
Letters make up words, words make up sentences, and sentences
make up concepts. It is a primarily linear construction that cannot be
easily rearranged without affecting meaning.

Photographs are representations of the physical world possessing a three-
dimensional sense of time and space. Photographs of landscapes feature a
horizon, while photographs of architecture have perspective and a vanishing
point. Portraits contain unique human features of eyes, nose, and mouth.
Each of these elements and scenarios commands a different point of entry
into a picture.

Unlike objects rendered in photographic space, letters and their forms do not
customarily exist in three-dimensional space. Letterforms themselves have no
intrinsic third dimension. Jan Tschichold, renowned typographer and designer, wrote a
wonderful metaphorical essay about working with type called "Clay in the Potter's Hand."
But type is less like clay and more like Legos. It is a prefabricated kit of parts, a closed
system, with typefaces whose inner harmonies make them complete in and of themselves.

A high-contrast
translation of the
poster emphasizes
how type space works
independently from
photographic space.

Contrast, Color, Texture:

While images render the world in a complete tonal range, tonal shifts generally interfere with,
more than contribute to, the clear reading of text. Type is therefore an inherently high-contrast
medium. Dieter Feseke of the Berlin-based studio umbra-dor observes, "The type is more geometry,
more digital and clean. The image is patchy, spotted, more analog, natural, and dirty." As the viewer
looks at and discovers a work that is formed of both entities, the flow of experience is varied, with
each medium dictating its own point of entry and rate of comprehension. The reading gets even more
intricate when the piece contains multiple images and text elements. Complexity adds to the time needed
to investigate and interpret a work, regulated by each viewer's level of experience. For intricacy to transcend
entanglement, designers must embrace the creative potential of photo-typographic space. These strategies
should guide the viewer beyond what Rick Poynor, in his book *No More Rules: Graphic Design and Postmodernism,*
calls "fully postmodern representational space, where all that is solid often melts into an intoxicating, semi-
abstract blur."

PROJECT
Poster: *Points of Access*
CLIENT
Grüntuch Ernst Architects
Berlin, Germany
DESIGNERS
Kerstin Baarmann,
Frank Döring,
and Dieter Feseke
umbra-dor/dor grafik
Berlin, Germany

In the poster, variations in color, scale, and rhythm in the typography aspire to achieve a unity between type and image.

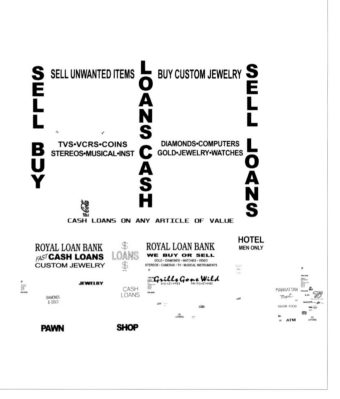

PROJECT
Untitled #26
PHOTOGRAPHER
Matt Siber
Chicago, USA

Overwhelmed by the intrusion of consumer culture on the urban landscape, photographer Matt Siber highlights this issue by literally detaching the text from the image. This approach dramatizes the two simultaneous but distinct ways of deciphering meaning within our everyday environment.

PROJECT
Poster: *Mother*
CLIENT
Self
STUDIO
David Tartakover
Tartakover Design
Tel Aviv, Israel
PHOTOGRAPHER
Jim Hollander
Reuters 1988

David Tartakover designed this poster around a newspaper photograph of a young Israeli soldier passing in front of a Palestinian woman. His placement of the single word *mother* (in stencil letters used by the army) in the doorway invites a universal connection that transcends politics.

MEANING

As containers for meaning and expressions of human experience, type and image have different properties—but they also operate on different levels of cognition.

Images open the door to multiple interpretations through varied experiences and memories. These connections make photography a more complex, and more visceral form of communication. Unlike images, words are essentially shapes that have learned, recognized meanings. Willi Kunz describes this phenomenon in *Typography: Macro- and Microaesthetics:* "Every word is comprised of a particular set of letters, whose sequence and form makes each word semantically and syntactically unique."

The work on the pages that follow is in many different languages, reminding us very clearly that words are forms that communicate only to those who understand the specific code of that language. Words, while potentially harboring some ambiguities based on exposure and additional learned references, are a more explicit form of communication.

When type meets image, there is automatically a dialogue between them and each can pull the other in many different directions.

The text can support or contradict the image just as the image can illustrate or refute the written message. Each may also contain independent meanings that may react with or against the overall message in the work. To compound the interpretation further, additional relationships can spring up from the viewers' backgrounds and personal points of view.

In his essay "The Photographic Message," Roland Barthes said of the interaction of text and image: "It is true that there is never a real incorporation since the substances of the two structures (graphic and iconic) are irreducible, but there are most likely degrees of amalgamation."

During the process of analyzing the photo-typographic works contained in these pages, the difficulty of teasing out the visual from the verbal brought the struggle between the two forms of communication to the forefront. It is impossible to construct an authentic written description of the type/image relationship at work in a piece of visual communication. For, in order to measure that dynamic completely, one has to go to a place in the mind that doesn't speak or explain, but rather absorbs. These examples are rare because they take you there.

FOUR CRITICAL RELATIONSHIPS

When type and image coexist, each remains a distinguishable entity, occupying its own space and time to greater and/or lesser degrees, while continuously interacting in distinct ways. Though the combinations of permutations of type and image are infinite, the integration of these media can be delineated according to the following criteria:

separation
when the type and image
operate independently

fusion
when the type and image
blend to form a unity

fragmentation
when the type and image
disturb or disrupt each other

inversion
a form of *fusion,* when the
type and image trade places
and the type takes on pictorial
properties or the image takes
on typographic qualities

This workshop is focused primarily on poster design as a form because posters transcend and propel layout into a realm where type and image can combine seamlessly. In poster design, words and pictures step out of the compositional boundaries and workaday responsibilities that often distance them in conventional page layout.

All four interactions—*separation, fusion, fragmentation,* and *inversion*—manifest themselves both formally and pragmatically. Designers can use them for many purposes as well as to create a range of visual effects. The practical applications reviewed here include: to present and clarify facts, to tell a story, to persuade, to express emotion, or to create an atmosphere.

Separation is the starting point because it allows a more in-depth introduction into how words and pictures function independently. Then it will be easier to recognize the blending forces of *fusion,* and the disruptive nature of *fragmentation. Inversion,* the final section, is divided into *Type as Image* and *Image as Type.*

In discussing each interaction, we will break down the categories even more, to investigate how designers direct type and image combinations to reinforce a message or idea. A single design often contains many of these relationships; however, for this workshop, discussion will be focused on analyzing examples of graphic design as they have been placed in the category for which they have the strongest affinity.

SEPARATION

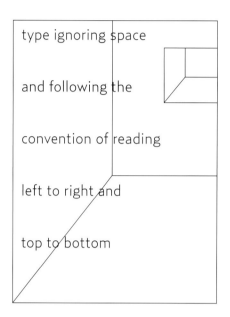

type ignoring space

and following the

convention of reading

left to right and

top to bottom

FUSION

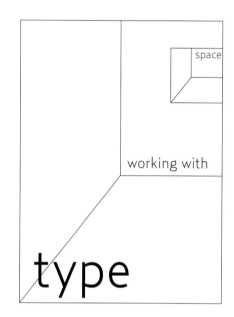

space

working with

type

FRAGMENTATION

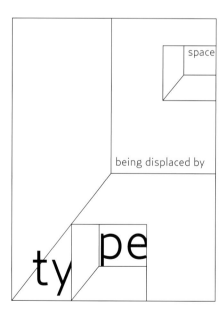

space

being displaced by

type

INVERSION

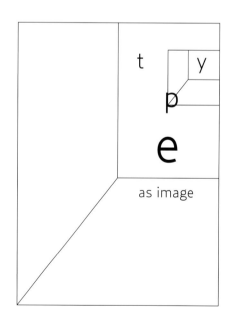

type

as image

Diagrams showing the four critical relationships between typographic space and photographic space. (The photographic image is represented by the line drawing.)

While they are illustrated here as stand-alone scenarios, it is important to keep in mind that more than one of these conditions may exist in any given piece.

SEPARATION

Type and image operate independently

In this chapter we'll examine many different kinds of type/image relationships that fall under the category of separation. By applying the principle of separation, text and image retain a clear level of autonomy; the designer allows the text to react with, against, or independently from the image. Often the designer inserts additional graphic elements that further mediate the type and image.

Applications

To play the type against the image

To reinforce the message

To contradict the message

To invite multiple meanings

When type and image exist separately, the viewer can read or connect two (or more) distinct messages.

To create a series

Designating a consistent frame or space to contain the text creates a unifying system to call out the identity of a sponsoring organization, allowing it to stand apart from the expressive description of a specific event (e.g., lecture, concert, film).

To provide clarity

To delineate a structure and hierarchy for the presentation of complex information, such as event schedules, within the context of images

Formal qualities

Layering

The type is superimposed on the image but remains distinct from the image.

Border or Frame

A border or frame contains the type and sets the stage for the photograph.

Compartments or Windows

The picture plane is divided into type spaces and image spaces.

This poster series for Radio France captures the potential for theme and variations that can be sustained by the use of a strong interchangeable type and image format. These posters illustrate the concept of layering as well as framing. A silhouetted human form is employed as an outline, taking the viewer through the range of possibilities for each concert; and on a deeper level, suggesting the transformation one feels while listening to music.

SEPARATION

FIGURES DE CLAVIERS
14-15-16 décembre

les
concerts
de
radio
france
2001
2002

RadioFrance

The layered secondary images do not literally illustrate the themes of the concerts but merely suggest them, inviting viewers to derive the message.

PROJECT
Invitations and posters for concert series:
Les Concerts de Radio France
CLIENT
Radio France
Paris, France
DESIGNER
Anette Lenz
Atelier Anette Lenz
Paris, France

This diagram shows the elements that remain constant. The type, positioned off the bottom of the foot, appears to be almost dancing with the figure.

The visual theme is played out for many programs of the concert season. Opposite: *figures de claviers*, and clockwise from top: *figures de femmes (women)*, *figures de poésie (poetry)*, *figures légères (light)*, *figures antiques (antiques)*.

It is important to note that the format, while displaying different background patterns and layered secondary images, maintains a consistent relationship between the text and the "dancing" figure. It is this alliance that reinforces the strong identity of the series.

In these two compositions to promote a theatrical presentation, the designer has created the sense of separate environments, layered and intertwined. Partly reflective, partly interwoven, at the same time they stand apart. Image and text can be read separately, but they clearly depend on each other to convey the complete visual message.

SEPARATION

This poster series, with its illusory orthographic structure, employs geometry to block out a pathway for the type and image to interact.

PROJECT
Invitations and posters
for theater series
CLIENT
Théâtre d'Angoulême
Angoulême, France
DESIGNER
Anette Lenz
Vincent Perrottet
Paris, France

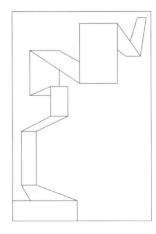

Diagram showing the
ribbon structure.
The banded architecture
of the format remains
constant, but the
application of a new
image generates a
completely new design.

A geometric "ribbon" contrasts with the organic natural forms of the images, allowing the text space to locate itself comfortably within the framework. The message is clear and well defined, but it still energizes the overall composition.

Through a system of mirroring one image into a series of oblique compartments, the designer has invited the viewer into a multi-dimensional space that moves beyond that of the original single image. The poster leads the imagination into another world where possibilities continually unfold for reading and contemplating the message.

Anette Lenz created further multiplicity in the images while keeping the words clear and distinctly separated in her designs of a series of posters and postcards for the annual season of the Théâtre d'Angoulême. The visual theme of this series is played out with a range of photographs mirrored along various axes to create a kaleidoscopic effect, resulting in a lively tension between cohesion and variation.

SEPARATION

Landscape mixes with type to form a floating composition of information and image.

PROJECT
Invitations and posters for theater series
CLIENT
Théâtre d'Angoulême
Angoulême, France
DESIGNER
Anette Lenz
Vincent Perrottet
Paris, France

The geometry of these configurations makes the familiar suddenly unfamiliar, giving the viewer a new and more complex experience of space, both recognizable and unusual, leading to further investigation and discovery.

In an invitation for a series of children's theater programs (opposite), the designer transformed a soft landscape of trees and sky into a recognizable, playful characterization of a cat. Trees are reflected along a bilateral axis to form the shape of a cat face, which is further defined by two graphic eyes and "whiskers" of symmetrically placed text.

The second two invitations illustrate how layers can be changed to create different approaches to presenting the message. One (below left) allows the type to integrate within the landscape of the "mirrored" images while maintaining its separate layer and message. The other (below right) through increased levels of layering, displays its message as if through a window. The text is used almost as a "stencil" through which the viewer both reads and experiences the space.

Duplicating the geometry of the rows and aisles in the theater sets up a mesmerizing rhythm that invites the type to participate.

An additional layer of typographic information is ghosted over the image to further activate the space and suggest the vitality of the theater.

A high-contrast black-and-white diagram of the poster shows the intersections of the type space and image space.

SEPARATION

This poster for the Karl Blossfeldt exhibition shows how graphic notations of the photographic space form a framework for the type, which both complements the image and provides separation and legibility.

PROJECT
Poster for Karl Blossfeldt exhibition
CLIENT
Bauhaus Dessau Foundation
Dessau, Germany
DESIGNERS
Daniela Haufe and Detlef Fiedler
cyan
Berlin, Germany

In this poster for an exhibition of the early twentieth-century photographer and sculptor Karl Blossfeldt, the designers have structured a composite landscape of the artist's botanical photographs, and overlaid a progression of solid vertical rules aligned with the stems and leaves. The level of graphic abstraction is reminiscent of the style of design that originated at the Bauhaus building where the exhibit is taking place.

Even though both type and image are aligned in the space, there is still a beautiful honesty in the stark contrast between the organic, curvilinear forms in the plants and the more rigid geometric structure of the text. The grid arrangement of the text mimics a landscape in a more abstracted sense with the placement of the exhibition title, "Fotografie Stiftung Bauhaus Dessau," defining the horizon of a panoramic space. This sets the stage for a lively integration of the photographic and the graphic.

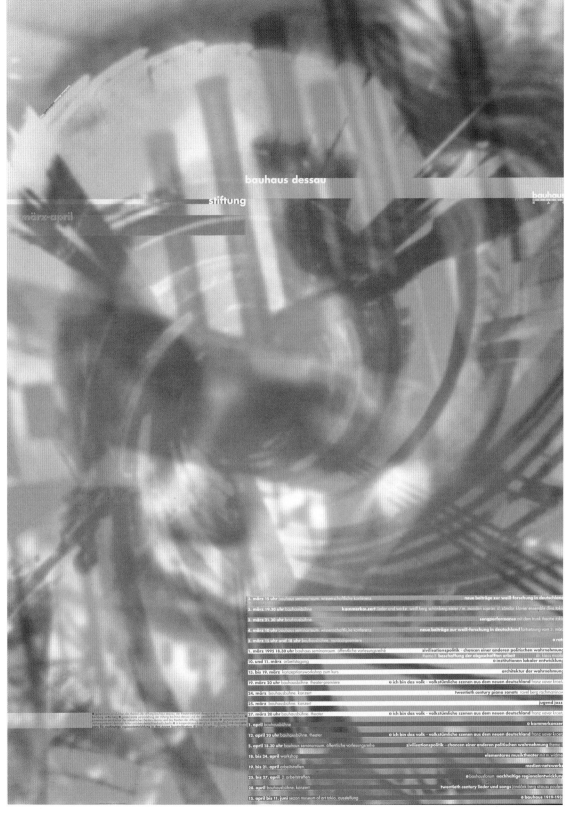

bauhaus dessau

stiftung

bauhaus

märz-april

Past and present are
layered to highlight the
current activities at
the Bauhaus Dessau
Foundation. Contrast
is key in defining and
harmonizing type
and image.

PROJECT
Monthly program calendar
CLIENT
Bauhaus Dessau
Foundation
Dessau, Germany
DESIGNERS
Daniela Haufe and
Detlef Fiedler
cyan
Berlin, Germany

This is one poster from a calendar series for the Bauhaus Dessau Foundation that is based on a system of layering type and image from the past and present. Blending historic and recent photographs, this composition encapsulates the feeling of time, place, and spirit of the creative forces at work within the Bauhaus both now and historically. The viewer is made strongly aware, through the use of montage, of a sense of motion—of moving forward through layers of time.

The text maintains a separate and unified position in the lower right corner of the composition, supported on a structure of strong horizontal rules. A woman's face is layered with a photograph of an industrial construction. (Note the formal relationship between the structure of the blades within the overlaid turbine photograph, and the use of horizontal stripes, supporting the text.)

In the spirit of the musical event for which it was composed, this poster captures both the structure and energy of sound. This quality is achieved through the blending of two images, a fire escape and an abstract illusion of light rays. The grillwork of the fire escape generates a related structure—a solid blue framework that contains the type on a layer that rises to the foreground. The layers are distinct—one soft-focus and one hard and graphic—and yet integrated, with corresponding intervals and placements that echo the musical theme. Unlike the distortion in the photographic fire escape, which appears in perspective, the typographic grid is flat and operates at right angles to the picture plane. This further defines the location of the type and separates it from the image.

SEPARATION

PROJECT
Poster for chamber
concert
CLIENT
Bauhaus Dessau
Foundation
Dessau, Germany
DESIGNERS
Daniela Haufe and
Detlef Fiedler
cyan
Berlin, Germany

Music is suggested by
layers of type, graphic
elements, and photography
in this poster for a concert
at the Bauhaus Dessau.

Another in a series of monthly program posters, this piece (shown below left) also layers elements to invoke past and present: the history of the Bauhaus and information about current programs at the school. The background layer is an assemblage of nostalgic photographs, including multiple images of an antique doll. A web of orange light is woven throughout the space, setting up a middle layer. The text, which both summarizes Bauhaus history and lists current events at the school, appears in broad horizontal bands spanning the width of the poster. Each band is split into two columns, the left one offering information in German and the right one, in English.

This poster (below right) is another by cyan for an exhibition at the Bauhaus in Dessau titled "Mag Mec Berlin" of plans and models for futuristic department stores designed by architecture students in Rosenheim. The structural underpinning for this layered composition is a map that contains exhibition details and related information. Other elements are suspended—illustrations of airplanes and a helicopter above, and a ghostlike human figure below, the map layer. It is remarkable that even though these various elements float separately on their own layers, the final composition is beautifully integrated.

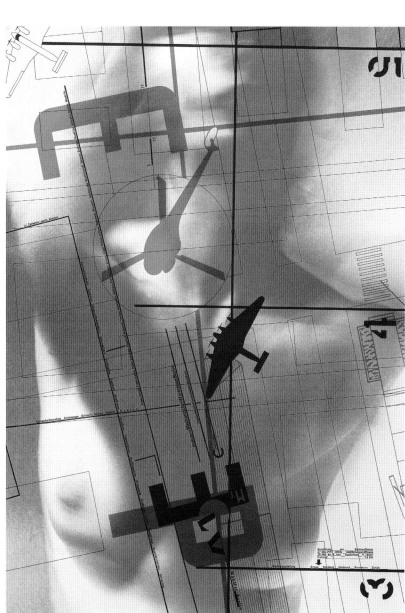

PROJECT
Monthly program poster
CLIENT
Bauhaus Dessau
Foundation
Dessau, Germany
DESIGNERS
Daniela Haufe and
Detlef Fiedler
cyan
Berlin, Germany

The past and present ambience of the Bauhaus is reconfigured with layers of image and type in cyan's monthly program poster.

A map acts as a mediating layer, or grid, between soft-focus photography and crisp graphic elements.

PROJECT
Poster for Mag Mec
exhibition
CLIENT
Bauhaus Dessau
Foundation
Dessau, Germany
DESIGNERS
Daniela Haufe and
Detlef Fiedler
cyan
Berlin, Germany
PHOTOGRAPHER
Daniela Haufe

This poster, created to announce a summer exhibition schedule at the Bauhaus, is reminiscent of early photographic techniques that were developed at the school. Close-up portraits, double exposed with strong architectural elements, suggest a connection between the place itself and the human personalities that inhabited the institution.

SEPARATION

An image of a serene woman tinted in lavender melts into a bright red image of structural, architectural elements. The text layer comes forward in white.

PROJECT
Summer program poster
CLIENT
Bauhaus Dessau
Foundation
Dessau, Germany
DESIGNERS
Daniela Haufe and
Detlef Fiedler
cyan
Berlin, Germany

Strong angular gestures arranged in a symmetrical composition support the message of theatrical drama in this poster for winter exhibitions and performances at the Bauhaus. Here multiple exposures are anchored by a rigid cruciform text arrangement to achieve a sense of activity and interaction. The textured overlay adds further energy and color to the surface of the poster. The position of the text conforms to the symmetry in the background image and further layers the composition by making a "window" in the space. Running the text to the edge of the box further elevates the ambiguity between the layers.

Dark tones in the background set the stage for this theatrical composition for the winter season.

PROJECT
Winter program poster
CLIENT
Bauhaus Dessau
Foundation
Dessau, Germany
DESIGNERS
Daniela Haufe and
Detlef Fiedler
cyan
Berlin, Germany

Separation not only allows for texts to stand isolated but can also accommodate graphic patterns to further mediate the text and the accompanying images. In this poster for an exhibition of contemporary British art in Berlin, the pattern presents itself almost as a code system asking the viewer to decipher it to complete the reading of the message.

In a formal sense, the layer of dots tends to flatten the three-dimensionality of the photographic space, creating a curtain for the viewer to penetrate for further details and messages below its surface.

PROJECT
**Poster for UK
art exhibition**
CLIENT
**The British Council
London, UK**
DESIGNERS
**Daniela Haufe and
Detlef Fiedler
cyan
Berlin, Germany**
PHOTOGRAPHER
Jeremy Murch

SEPARATION

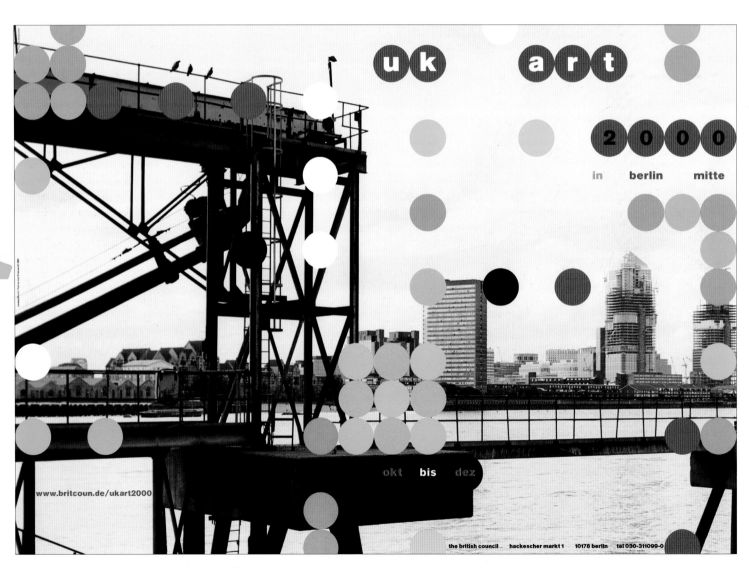

A layer of dots locates the text and creates an optical curtain between the viewer and the image in this poster by cyan for an exhibition of British art.

PROJECT
Twentieth anniversary
poster
CLIENT
*Freunde guter Musik
(Friends of Good Music)*
Berlin, Germany
DESIGNERS
Daniela Haufe and
Detlef Fiedler
cyan
Berlin, Germany

This vibrant illustration
both integrates the text
and keeps it separate
to promote this concert of
contemporary music.

This illustration of a residential interior (top left) attempts to mimic a "real" photographic space using pattern and color as the primary language for communicating the message. The text becomes present as pictures on a wall, almost completely integrated but at times slightly out of perspective—and thus maintaining a distinct separation from the image. The whimsical use of bright color further adds to the 1950s nostalgia that the composition conveys. Instead of placing the viewer in a public space, such as an actual concert hall, this symbolic rendering of a personal living space opens up a more private connection between the audience and the music.

The strong optical pattern in this poster (bottom left) suggests the nature of an electronic performance. The text is supported by rectangular structures floating above the waves. Each is isolated, but the viewer cannot escape the sense that there are three distinct layers at work here, not just two. The pattern itself occupies the background; the transparent rectangle on the left forms the middle layer, and solid text blocks define a top layer. The middle layer, or transparent color, acts as a buffer between the intensity of the vibration produced by the background image and the need for legibility in the type.

Optical art lays the
foundation for a
minimalist composition
of colored fields to convey
the sensation of listening
to electronic music.

PROJECT
Poster: *Suite in Parochial*
CLIENT
Kunst in Parochial
DESIGNERS
Daniela Haufe and
Detlef Fiedler
cyan
Berlin, Germany

For a season of plays at the Théâtre Les Gémeaux in Paris, Michel Bouvet created a unique black and white poster for each production, distilling the plots into simplified images. Here the poster format becomes a stage upon which each symbolic object depicts specific characters, emotional attachments, or concepts.

A distinctive framing device is used throughout the series of posters, reinforcing the theme of staging. Expressive variations in the titling text operate independently within the frame of each composition to further define the character of each play. This text takes many forms, transforming it from straightforward information into a typographic voice offering clues about the emotional nature of the performances. Les Gémeaux's logo and essential information consistently appear along the left margin of the frame, adding to the strong series identity.

PROJECT
Series of theater posters
CLIENT
Les Gémeaux
Sceaux, France
DESIGNER
Michel Bouvet
Paris, France
PHOTOGRAPHER
Francis Laharrague
Fréjus, France

In this poster for *Maison de Poupée (A Doll's House)*, Bouvet montaged the head of a doll onto an image of a mansion to portray Nora, a housewife struggling for independence within the confines of her traditional lifestyle.

Early sketches (right) show how Bouvet's conceptual process begins with the image.

A consistent framing device helps maintain a strong series identity (above).

A simple triangle of nails represents the risk of punishment for unlawful sexual activity that is central to the plot of Shakespeare's *Measure for Measure*.

An image of a crumpled, broken bugle acts as a metaphor for Don Juan's exploits in *Don Juan Returns from the War*.

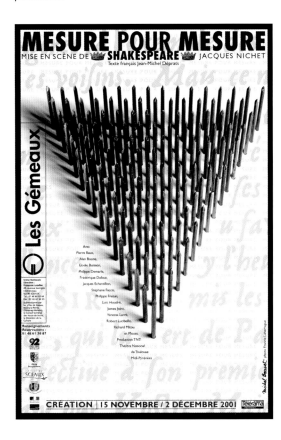

A close-up photograph of a severed rope represents the broken rope bridge in Thornton Wilder's *Bridge of San Luis Rey* (right).

A key cut from hide symbolizes the powers of the magic skin in Balzac's story "La peau de chagrin" (The Magic Skin). A label attached to the key contains the name of the play—making the type part of the image (far right).

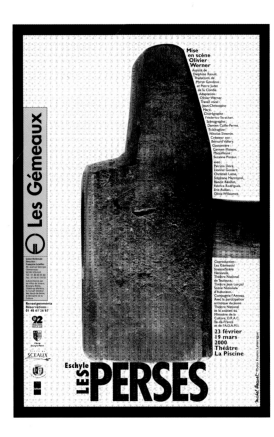

A stone weapon represents *Les Perses* (*The Persians*), an ancient Greek tragedy about the Persian Wars (far left).

The "stone-faced" image in the poster for Ibsen's play *Les Revenants* (*Ghosts*) symbolizes the memory of the deceased husband. There is also ghosted type in the title (left).

The dramatic irony of Sophocles' timeless tragedy *Oedipe le Tyran* (*Oedipus the King*) is emphasized through the combination of the broken heart of glass and the dagger-shaped title.

The central image of this poster for the play *Alexandria Quartet* is a die with a four on every side to represent Lawrence Durrell's book in which the same story is seen and told by four different people.

Initial sketches experimenting with the idea of four points of view.

Bouvet clearly understands the power of the black-and-white photograph—it is more immediately abstract, yet still capable of revealing the detail within each subject. The images convey strength, and when used as they are here for posters in the streets of Paris, can stand out on even the most crowded kiosks.

Themes of vulnerability and lack of self-awareness are depicted in this poster for two plays by Anton Chekhov, *La mouette (The Seagull)* and *Ivanov.*

In these self-published works, Jonathan Barnbrook presents a personal political viewpoint and invites a public response. He takes the design concept of separation a step further by substituting an empty window where the viewer would expect to see text. By offering the opportunity for the viewer to complete the message, the poster series becomes "interactive," allowing for multiple interpretations (the public viewpoint). However, Barnbrook's choice of font for the name of each political figure and his use of a cartoonish "speech bubble" provides some substantial evidence of his own point of view.

SEPARATION

WHAT SHOULD BUSH REALLY BE SAYING?

FILL IN ABOVE

"What Should Bush Really Be Saying?" is one of a series of posters inviting the viewer to "fill in the blank" and question the honesty of the president's intentions.

PROJECT
Series of political posters
CLIENT
Self
DESIGNER
Jonathan Barnbrook
Barnbrook Design
London, UK

The transposition of letters that puts the word *liar* in Blair's name brings into question Tony Blair's integrity.

The tension between what politicians say and what they do is reinforced in this poster of Kim Jong II of North Korea.

Here, word and image work together to imply a simple yet powerful connection between the Secretary General of the United Nations Kofi Annan and the United States of America.

Thick black rules animate the message and mediate the separation of type and image in this poster about human values, done for the organization Secours Populaire Français by Pierre Bernard.

PROJECT
Poster about Human Values
CLIENT
Secours Populaire Français
Paris, France
DESIGNER
Pierre Bernard
Atelier de Création Graphique
Paris, France

Separation of type and image facilitates the reading of two messages—a before and after—in this poster (opposite) encouraging respect and human dignity, designed by Pierre Bernard for the humanitarian organization Secours Populaire Français. Here the typography becomes interactive—playing two different messages against a complex assemblage of images in order to emphasize both the personal and ethical issues at stake. The words—*inégalité* (inequality), *exclusion, injustice*—are still legible even though crossed out and replaced with words expressing new sentiments: *respect, dévouement* (devotion), *solidarité*. The same style of heavy black rules cross out the "old" words and underline the "new." The backdrop for this transformation is a collage indicative of family snapshots as well as a large dove that symbolizes the organization.

In a unique example of separation, designer Peter Moser used an actual police crime scene photograph in a poster announcing an exhibition at the Museum für Gestaltung in Zurich. The poster showing just the crime scene (below left) was displayed on kiosks for two days—they contained no text to explain their purpose. Viewers were left to ponder the mystery and draw their own conclusions. Two days later an X of yellow tape with the title of the show, "Scene" and its venue was applied to each poster (below right), solving the mystery for viewers.

PROJECT
Poster for art exhibition:
Scene of the Crime
CLIENT
Museum für Gestaltung
Zurich, Switzerland
DESIGNER
Peter Moser
Velvet Creative Office
GmbH
Lucerne, Switzerland

Velvet Creative Office took the principle of separation to an extreme, first exhibiting a poster with minimal typography and then later adding "crime scene" tape containing text.

SEPARATION

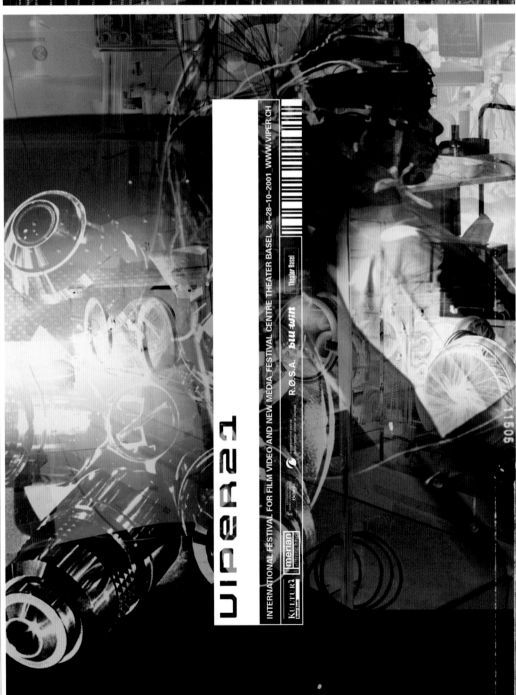

The folding poster/flier
for the Viper Film Festival
surrounds designated
white space for type
information with
photographic ambience.

PROJECT
Poster/flier and catalog
for Viper 2001
International Festival for
Film, Video, and
Multimedia
CLIENT
Viper International
Festival
Basel, Switzerland
DESIGNER
Peter Moser
Velvet Creative Office
GmbH
Lucerne, Switzerland

The influences of film and new media are encapsulated within the poster and catalog for the Viper International Festival. Image montage, vibrant color combinations, and a varying selection of text fonts combine to add a level of energy that frame the articles and schedules on each page. By separating the text from the image in white fields, the designers have made all the necessary information clear and unimpeded. This system of white titling bands and text boxes appears in all the materials, including posters, covers, and interior pages.

The festival catalog cover and interior pages follow the same type and image strategy but use warm colors for the images.

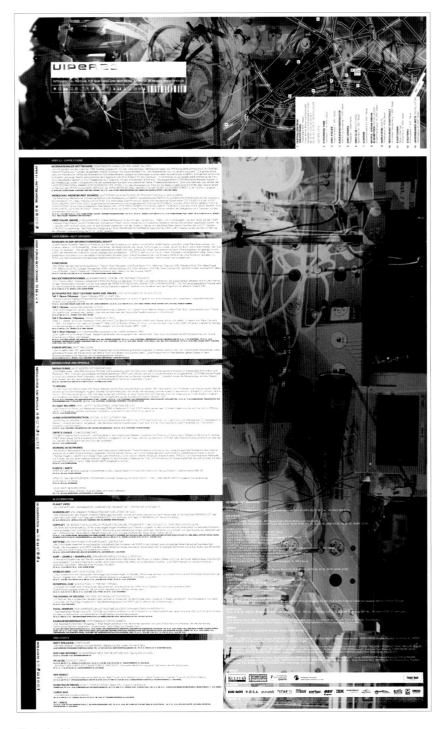

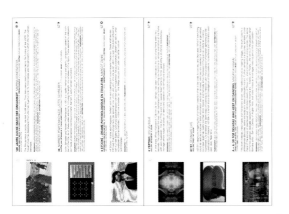

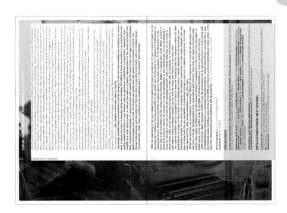

TYPE, IMAGE, MESSAGE

The back of the poster shows how the piece can be folded and used as a flier. Again, all text is on a white field.

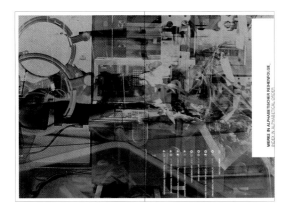

In the fourteenth century Chinese play *Peony Pavilion (The Return of the Soul)*, one of the main settings is the heroine's family garden. Accordingly, the designers have chosen a garden as the primary source of the imagery in this poster (below left). One of the central themes in the play is that of transformation, from life to death and back to life. By superimposing images of both barren plants and fully leaved trees, this composition depicts that cycle.

The title appears both in English and Chinese. The English title is placed horizontally across the upper third of the poster, emphasizing the idea of land (earth). The Chinese title, located vertically adjacent to the right edge, positions itself in the plantings (nature). By choosing to reinforce the concepts in the images with the text arrangement, the designers have given the viewer much to reflect on prior to seeing the performance.

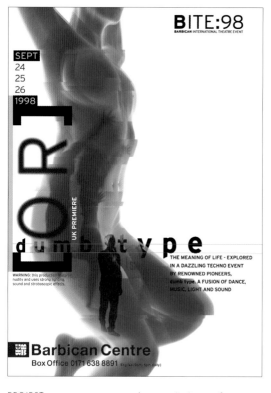

PROJECT
Poster: *Peony Pavilion*
CLIENT
Barbican Centre
London, UK
DESIGNER
Why Not Associates
London, UK

Why Not Associates' poster for *Peony Pavilion* evokes a meditative atmosphere for a Chinese love story. Two kinds of type are interacting with the image—Roman letterforms and Chinese characters.

PROJECT
Poster: *OR*, a multimedia performance
CLIENT
Barbican Centre
London, UK
DESIGNER
Why Not Associates
London, UK

A composite image of human forms exerts its presence in relation to the type in this poster for an international theater event.

To capture the "fusion of dance, music, light, and sound" in this "techno" performance, a progression of superimposed human figures creates an extremely energetic image (above right). The blue color further enhances the abstract qualities and extreme experimental nature of the event. Through the use of vivid red and black type in a strong vertical orientation, the main title stands out against this highly charged image.

"An Exploration of Views and Perceptions of the Body" is the description for *Scan,* a dance performance by choreographer Rosemary Butcher. The production incorporates live dancers, lighting effects, sound, and film to create an all-encompassing energetic atmosphere. "Externalizing the internal through light, image, and movement" are the words on the invitation. The designers chose to capture these ideas by using X-rays of the human body (the internal) in combination with silhouettes of dancers (the external). The type is choreographed in unexpected and highly experimental arrangements, working in formation with and against the images to achieve a provocative and highly lyrical effect.

The use of color is explored to its fullest on the poster (below) and somewhat "tamed" on the invitation (at right, top and bottom). The urban street context for the poster requires an elevated presence, whereas the invitation, viewed closer, requires clarity.

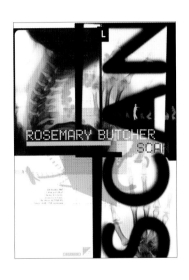

Poster: Rosemary
Butcher's *Scan*
CLIENT
University of Sussex
Brighton, UK
DESIGNER
Why Not Associates
London, UK

By separating the text from a multicolored image into a series of white bands, the designer has maintained clarity and readability while adding an uplifting gesture.

PROJECT
**Poster for choral concert:
Sergei Rachmaninov's
*Vespers***
CLIENT
**St. Nikolai Church Choir
of the State Tretyakov
Gallery
Moscow, Russia**
DESIGNER
**Yuri Gulitov
Moscow, Russia**

In the poster shown opposite, Designer Yuri Gulitov elegantly separated the essential concert information in white from the religious iconography of the church dome to maintain the mood of an evening choral program. The text seems to float, ascending upward into the dome, like music—completing the composition and signifying the spiritual elevation one might feel when attending the concert.

With the words *reflection begins* on the left and *reflection ends* on the right, Allen Hori sets up a challenging dichotomy for the viewer to ponder (below). The structure gives little clue to the designer's true purpose. Horizontal and symmetrical, it is absent of color, except in the center portion with its dominant red background, red tulip, and lone yellow flower. The photograph of the field, taken by the designer and "recycled" from an earlier photographic series, leads to speculation that the observer is at the starting point of a long journey.

In this promotional piece designed by Allen Hori, the text is inserted on either side of the composition, on "signposts" that define the possible directions (choices) and are the only clues to the events about to unfold.

PROJECT
Self-promotional poster
CLIENT
Bates Hori
New York, USA
DESIGNER
Allen Hori
Bates Hori
New York, USA

When asked about the process for designing with type and image and which he considers first, Peter Moser, who works with a team of ten people, stated, "How to start is a work in process for the whole team. It depends on what the work is all about....In the first more conceptual phase we try to find the key to it, then in the second phase, we create the [primary] visual elements and then allow the type to find its place."

PROJECT
Fashion catalog
CLIENT
Hillschwab
DESIGNER
Peter Moser
Velvet Creative Office
GmbH
Lucerne, Switzerland

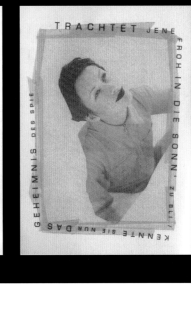

This project for the Swiss fashion label Hillschwab illustrates the team's process at work. Sequencing photographs of models wearing the featured clothing, the designers selected both close-up (subjective), and full-length (objective) imagery and juxtaposed them with a Dada-inspired poetic text. The combination creates a rhythm for the entire piece, with the text forcing unexpected connections in the viewer's mind, and the imagery establishing a dramatic and surreal attitude.

"Image and type have to fit the idea of transformation, both and equal. Type and image have to become unique and one," Moser says. "They stand for the idea." These issues are made very clear within this project.

Seemingly random associations are made between a Dadaist text and a sequence of fashion images in these advertisements for the Hillschwab clothing collection.

In creating this series of three posters for a dual exhibition of African and Dadaist art, the designer has considered carefully the relationships between the two collections.

PROJECT
Poster for Han Coray Collections
CLIENT
Museo Cantonale d'Arte Lugano, Switzerland
DESIGNER
Bruno Monguzzi Meride, Switzerland

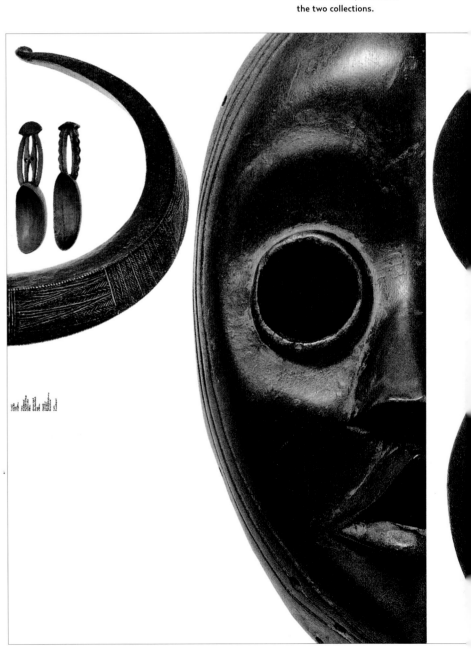

"The problem is to know what the problem is." This quote from designer Bruno Monguzzi sums up his methodology for seeking the best solution to difficult design challenges. In this case, the assignment was to publicize parallel exhibitions at the Museo Cantonale d'Arte in Lugano, Switzerland, for two of Han Coray's collections—African art and Dada. Sequencing, framing, proportion, and dramatic scale changes all contribute directly to the reading of this triptych. The selected pieces "dance"—first within their own spaces and then with the accompanying pieces. Although the scale changes in the text blocks echo the dynamic size shifts in the images, the type layer is significantly smaller and recedes into the background like a pulse supporting the more theatrical presence of the images.

The total result is a striking series presenting a beautifully structured, expressive unity. It clarifies, even for the casual passerby, the surprising harmony between Arp's central Dadaist sculpture and African art. Monguzzi has summed up his process by saying, "Communication is ultimately dealing with what you wish to happen in someone else's mind."

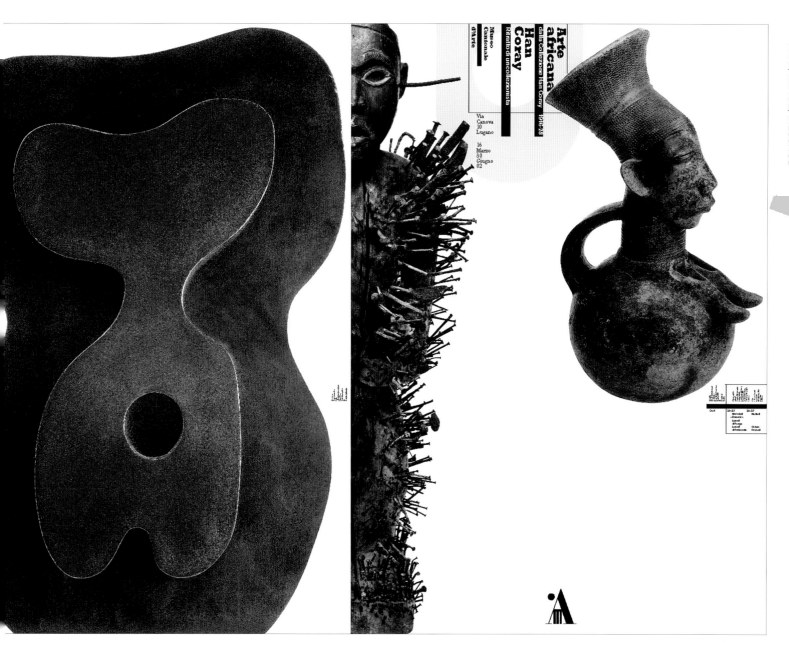

SEPARATION

Werner Jeker's poster
sets up a high-contrast
tension and separation
between type, image,
and message.

de Jon Fosse

Du 26 janvier au 18 février 2001

Traduction française: Terje Sinding

Mise en scène: Jacques Lassalle

Assistante à la mise en scène: Lucie Tiberghien

Décor: Géraldine Allier

Costumes: Dominique Chauvin

Eclairages: Frank Thévenon

Son: Daniel Girard

Avec: Jean Damien Barbin

Johanna Nizard

Marianne Basler

Philippe Lardaud

Marie-Paule Trystam

Un
jour
en
été

Vidy-L

PROJECT
Theatrical poster: *Un jour
en été* (A Summer's Day)
CLIENT
Théâtre de Vidy-Lausanne
Lausanne, Switzerland
DESIGNER
Werner Jeker
Les Ateliers du Nord
Lausanne, Switzerland

Werner Jeker is a master of type and image, using both with brilliant economy to create complex meaning. A soft-focus portrait fills this poster (opposite) for the play *A Summer's Day*. Through the use of a myopic central image, the designer paints a mysterious atmosphere upon which to place the text, and at the same time he skillfully ignites the viewer's curiosity about the performance.

By anchoring the main title on the left edge and placing the theater's name on the right, the designer sets up the opportunity for the creation of a text "bridge" containing the credits, dates, and location of the event. This text floats within the sight line of the person in the photograph. The strategic separation of text from image has made it possible to use an intimate type size, which invites the passerby to stop and read the essential information more closely. However, as the text comes into focus, the image becomes even more enigmatic.

Seductively simple, this poster (below left) promoting a new season of performances at the Théâtre de Vidy appears at first to be just a leaf and well-placed text information. However, as the viewer carefully considers the overall arrangement of objects on the expansive white surface, their proportion and color, it becomes increasingly obvious that the leaf can also be read as the mouth of a stage performer.

For an exhibition of photographs by the Lausanne photographer Luc Chessex, the designer assembled only a small sampling of the artist's work (below right) in order to hint at the nature of the presentation. The photographer, well known for his images of the Cuban revolution in the early 1960s, had assembled a large collection of images from his travels around the world. These powerful vignettes of life create an inspiring narrative that can only be suggested on the poster, but by scaling the primary text information to span the width of the piece, Werner Jeker has provided a grand gesture that both announces the exhibition and connotes the breadth of the photographer's work.

PROJECT
Theatrical poster:
Saison 2000–2001
CLIENT
Théâtre de Vidy-Lausanne
Lausanne, Switzerland
DESIGNER
Werner Jeker
Les Ateliers du Nord
Lausanne, Switzerland

A human face is suggested by the masterful arrangement of the text and the horizontal placement of the red leaf/ lips in this poster for the Théâtre de Vidy in Lausanne, Switzerland.

PROJECT
Poster for Luc Chessex exhibition
CLIENT
Musée des Arts Décoratifs
Lausanne, Switzerland
DESIGNER
Werner Jeker
Les Ateliers du Nord
Lausanne, Switzerland

In this poster the use of multiple images for an exhibition by Luc Chessex suggests the wide variety of photographs he has taken in his lifetime.

SEPARATION

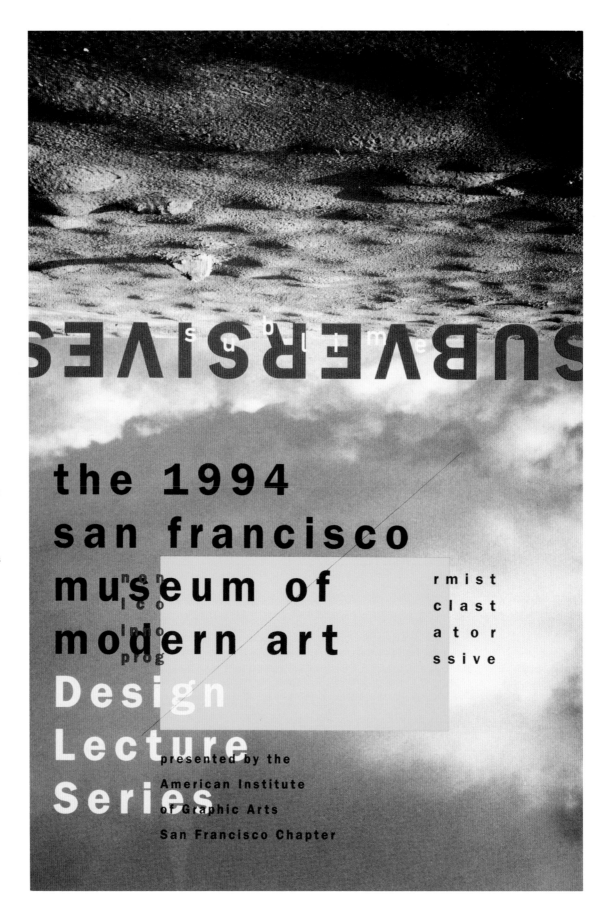

Because the image and type are operating separately, even more opportunity is opened up for interaction. To read the text on this postcard, the reader must literally turn it upside down.

PROJECT
Invitation postcards
CLIENT
AIA San Francisco
San Francisco, USA
DESIGNER
Lucille Tenazas
Tenazas Design
San Francisco, USA

Annual invitations designed by Lucille Tenazas for a lecture series at the San Francisco Museum of Modern Art compress a great deal of visual activation into a small space. A mere 6" × 9" (15.2 × 22.9 cm), they take the form of the postcard to a whole new level.

With type reading both horizontally and vertically, and images turned in contrary directions, these exquisitely crafted handheld compositions entice the viewer to turn them over and around to look at the designs from many different orientations.

Tenazas prefers to work with classic typefaces, believing they give her the flexibility to experiment freely with letterforms as modular objects in space. The simple sans serifs can withstand the numerous shifts in color, spacing, and scale that are demanded of them as they become their own architecture on the two-dimensional picture plane. A pioneer in the art of "layering," the designer has a sharp instinct for, and a deep understanding of, that illusion; she knows the precise point where the viewer perceives a shift. Sometimes a simple breach of a border, or a transgression allowing a word to spread freely across two distinct backgrounds instead of correspond with them, is just enough to create a layer.

Here a simple system of quadrants sets up a stable background; some images and type stay within a quadrant; some do not.

An eye from a classical Greek sculpture forms the focal point of this radial composition.

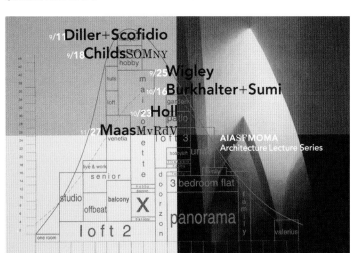

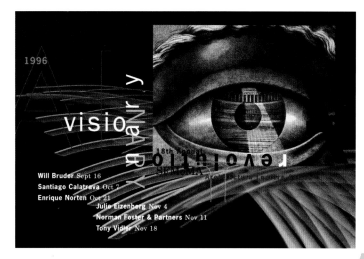

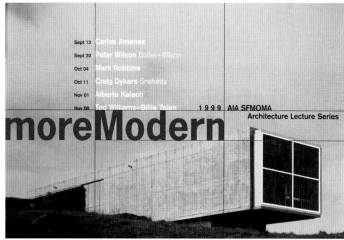

Columns of type run vertically to harmonize with the columns in the photograph. The space shifts from two-dimensional to three-dimensional, and the type, while staying "flat," reacts with and against the boundaries of the photographic and graphic elements.

A modular division of space, combined with asymmetrical image cropping, helps to emphasize the idea of simplicity for this lecture series titled "More Modern."

This poster for Musica Viva's performance series shows the unique use of vintage illustrations combined within a highly structured and well-organized picture plane.

PROJECT
Poster: *Musica Viva*
CLIENT
**Musica Viva
Munich, Germany**
DESIGN
**Günter Karl Bose
Berlin, Germany**

For this poster, Bose illustrated the idea of making a connection to the music by using a photograph of a wire extending from a coupling, which he placed within the frame created by the horizontal bands.

Each year, Musica Viva in Munich hosts a series of concerts featuring late twentieth- and early twenty-first century avant-garde music. The organization makes a special effort to introduce young composers and performers, in addition to featuring established experimental musicians.

Musica Viva challenged the designer Günter Karl Bose to produce a series of posters that would announce each year's performances in a highly imaginative way. The first issue Bose confronted was how to present the organization's identity. Musica Viva had no existing logotype, so he created a distinctive way to present the organization's name within the individual works. The concerts are performed only once, and only on a specified date. The designer turned this restriction into a feature of the design by making the day and month of the performances the largest text, and therefore the most easily recognized element, on each year's posters. In addition, for each year he developed a recognizable and supportive graphic language of images and a distinctive format.

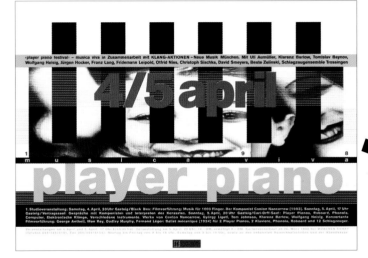

Here the designer implies the joy the audience will feel at the concert titled *Player Piano* with photos of happy faces behind a series of vertical graphic forms that suggest a piano keyboard.

For a performance by Olivier Messiaen, the designer used a photographic negative of pieces from a game board to convey the nature of the composer's work.

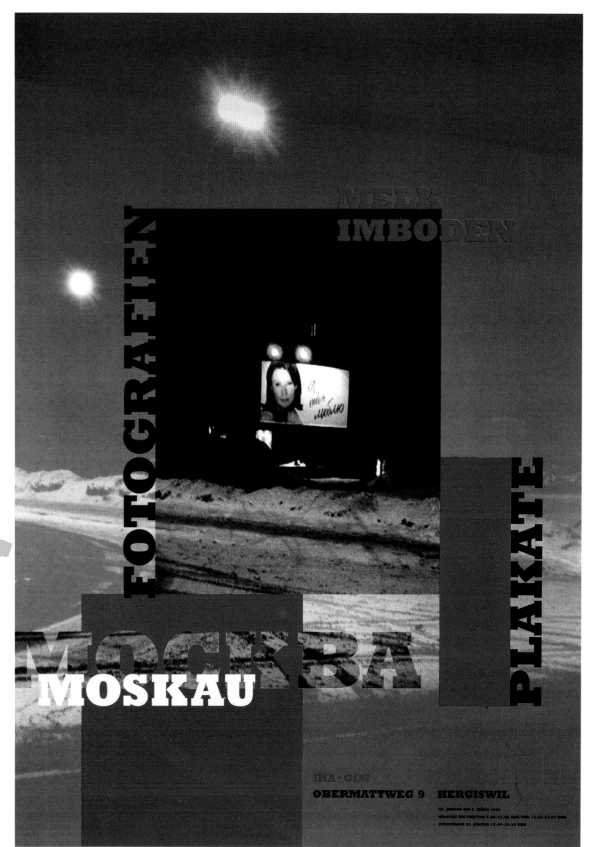

The designer Melk
Imboden layered a
number of framing
devices to add visual
impact and focus on
the photographic nature
of his work.

PROJECT
Poster for exhibition
CLIENT
Self
DESIGNER
**Melchior Imboden
Buochs, Switzerland**

For his poster exhibition in Moscow, the designer placed one of his photographs, of a winter's night on an isolated road, within the context of several framing devices. By first choosing to create a "window" layer, open in the middle and "frosted" on the outer section over the image, he allows only the innermost portion of the photograph to reveal itself distinctly. The primary text, *Fotografien Plakate,* appears to be cut from this portion of the window frame.

Red rectangles and larger text elements form additional layers, placed like building blocks, around the remaining central section. These devices call attention to the billboard image of a single human face, which is seemingly lost in this desolate landscape. The viewer's emotions cannot help but be stirred by the stark qualities of the composition.

Melk Imboden's poster for an exhibition of his photographs of jazz musicians (below left) is a striking, high-contrast composition. The grainy, luminous aura surrounding the head of the figure suggests the smoky, dark atmosphere of a jazz club. Only the essential elements are revealed—the profile of the face, with the mouthpiece of a saxophone, silhouetted against the glow of a single intense light source to provide a glimpse into the world of avant-garde saxophone player John Zorn, who is the subject of the portrait.

The title, *Jazzgesighter* (Jazz Seer), is set off in gold against the portrait on the black background. The text block is minimized, containing only the basic information: the museum and the dates of the exhibition. In this work, the designer has allowed the image to say almost everything.

A dynamic cruciform gesture dominates this work for the Luzern-Stans-Engelberg (LSE) rail line in Switzerland (below right). By using the strong single-point perspective of the photographic image, layering an equally powerful vertical line of informational text to divide the composition, and restricting the color palette to red, blue, and white, the designer has created memorable and visually arresting messages for his audience.

The sensation of movement in the photograph and the suggestion of a destination, as seen in the distant mountains, combine both the excitement and wonder of a travel experience into a single gesture.

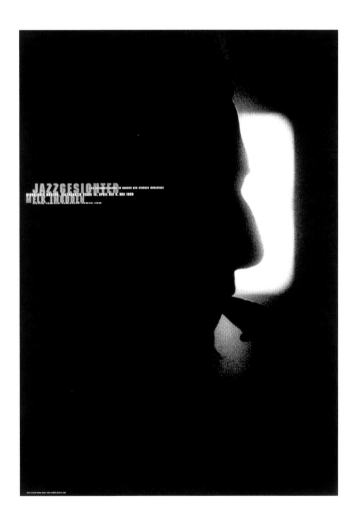

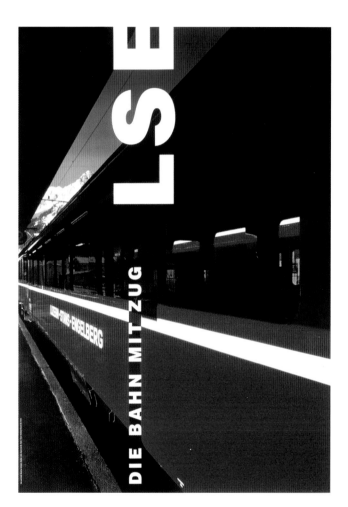

PROJECT
Poster for a
photographic exhibition
CLIENT
Nidwaldner Museum
Stans, Switzerland
DESIGNER
Melchior Imboden
Buochs, Switzerland

High contrast sets the
mood in this poster
for an exhibition of Melk
Imboden's jazz portraits.

PROJECT
Poster for LSE Rail
CLIENT
LSE Rail
Lucerne, Switzerland
DESIGNER
Melchior Imboden
Buochs, Switzerland

Melk Imboden's use of
a forced-perspective
photograph and
diametrically opposed
text creates a dynamic
composition for LSE
Railroad in Switzerland.

This series of highly abstract works could be characterized as the ultimate example of layering. Completed for the Kosaka-Giken Co., a general building consultancy in Japan, the photographic images of glasslike material create elegant compositions with a strong dynamic structure and a unique feeling of transparency.

The images are carefully composed assemblages of geometric forms, placed one on top of another, creating a series of picture planes that express a quiet energy and certainty of purpose. The same underlying system of layered gestures is the basis for the typographic arrangements, further emphasizing the idea of layering that is evident in all four works. When the posters are placed together, the viewer notices a subtle suggestion of the movement of time: the titles, positioned vertically or horizontally within their individual compositions, seem to become animated across the entire sequence.

With bold red symbols normally used for making survey maps on the top layer and direct, uncluttered imagery beneath, this diptych (opposite) prompts the viewer to ponder the meaning of the symbolism. The changing level of water in the glass indicates the passage of time, but is the glass being emptied or being filled? With these simple and elegant gestures, the designer has placed the emphasis on the nature of human consumption and its relationship to the natural environment. This is clearly a case where simplicity makes the strongest statement.

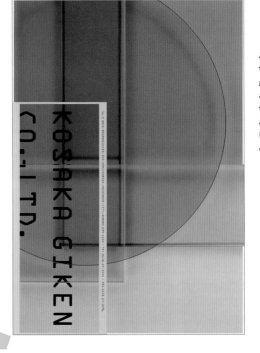

A system of layered transparent photographic gestures combined with a direct presentation of the text forms this highly abstract series for the Kosaka-Giken Co. of Japan.

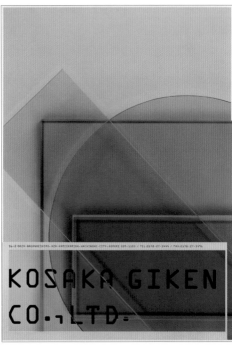

PROJECT
**Posters for a
building consultancy**
CLIENT
Kosaka Giken Co., Ltd.
DESIGNER
**Yasuhiro Sawada
Yasuhiro Sawada
Design Studio
Tokyo, Japan**

The designer combines
bold symbols with simple
and direct photographic
images to express ideas
on human consumption
and its relationship to
the natural environment.

These vibrant posters challenge the idea of a picture frame as a device to isolate and protect precious works of art. The reconfigured frames represent liberation from convention, changing points of view, and a redefining of the role of contemporary art in Japan.

The type is contained in a bright red "flag"—a relatively small floating element that moves with each new composition. The flag shape harmonizes with the image, but its vibrant red color and skewed angle make it stand out against the frames. The constants and variables all work together to reinforce the gallery's image as a place in a state of flux, accommodating many new approaches to art.

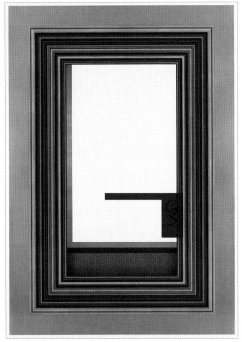

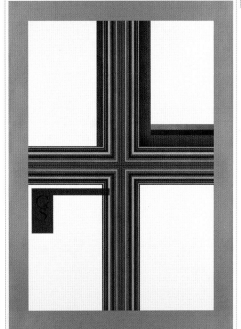

The unusually shaped
frames connote the idea
that the art in Gallery
Sugie is liberated from
traditional conventions.

PROJECT
Poster series for
Gallery Sugie
CLIENT
Gallery Sugie
Tokyo, Japan
DESIGNER
Yasuhiro Sawada
Yasuhiro Sawada
Design Studio
Tokyo, Japan

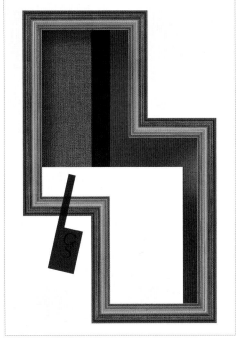

Using a sophisticated montage technique to imbed each poster with layers of meaning, Laboratories CCCP have produced these monumental posters. The images have been carefully constructed into pictorial icons that embody each theatrical event without disclosing the plot. The rich complexity of these images invites the audience to spend time decoding the images and drawing their own conclusions.

An image of an ear is nested in a rose that casts a pen nib shadow to symbolize a festival of lectures by prominent authors.

PROJECT
Theater posters
CLIENT
CDN Orléans Theater—Loiret-Centre Orléans, France
DESIGNER
Laboratories CCCP = Dr. Peche + Melle Rose Orléans, France

Centre Dramatique National / Orléans-Loiret-Centre

semaine des auteurs
Lectures suivies de rencontres avec les auteurs et les comédiens

Réservations au
02 38 81 01 00

PUR PRÉSENT

Thomas Bernhard   Ariane Gardel   Pascal Mainard   Benoît Guibert   Yann Apperry
Mardi - 20h30   Mercredi - 20h30   Jeudi - 19h   Vendredi - 19h   Samedi - 19h

16 17 18 19 20
mai 2000

Carré Saint-Vincent - Salles Antoine Vitez et le Kid

The letterforms, while clearly on a separate plane, have been modified to mimic—both in texture and color—the overall qualities of the pictures. The designers have coordinated their formal choices to reflect the character of each image, without sacrificing the legibility of the text. Text containing subordinate information, such as credits, times, and dates, is strategically located throughout the compositions and adds a sense of depth.

Color plays an important role in this duotone poster series. To underscore the meaning of each production, the creators adopted what could be considered a set of "conventional color codes," that is, a set of colors that have symbolism within the theater's cultural context. They used red, for example, to reinforce the image of the devil in *L'apocalypse Joyeuse* (Joyous Apocalypse), green to underscore the theme of money in *Tes*, and pink to add clarity to the rose for *Pur Présent* (Pure Present).

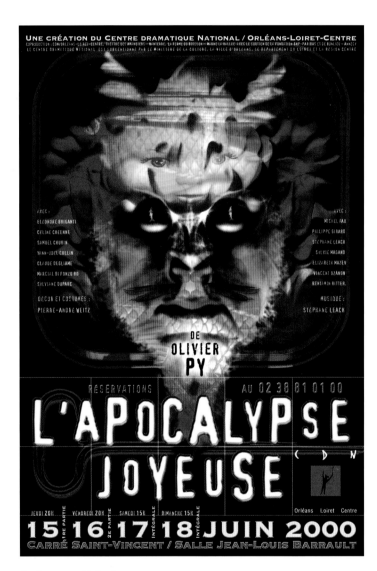

A unique assemblage of images from the play—a devil, a child, and a can of sardines—create an atmosphere of foreboding in this poster for *L'apocalypse Joyeuse* (The Joyous Apocalypse).

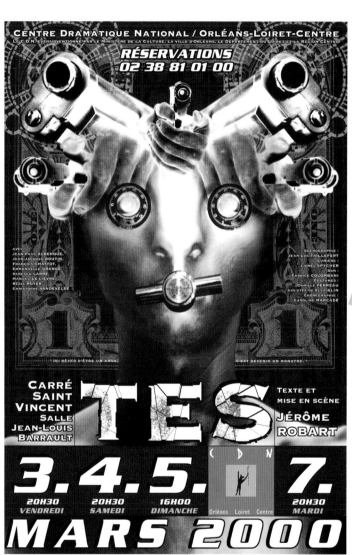

The designers have created the mythical character Tes, a bank robber, in a play based on the Minotaur's myth.

FUSION

Type and image merge into one entity

With fusion, a unifying force synthesizes the type and the image. Here the alliance of form and meaning presents itself in a strong visual coherence—a "cause and effect"—that is immediately apparent to the viewer. Some images and text are optically altered, and others are circumstantial through motion or juxtaposition, but they are all the result of deliberate, holistic choices made by the designer. Like a poem, fusion transforms experiences and concepts through careful craft and technique.

Formal qualities

Optical effect: perspective, lens, or filter

Type and image are connected in space by the use of perspective, a shared vanishing point, or an optical lens or filter.

Shared surface or texture

Type and image are woven into the texture of, or adhered to, a unifying surface—either the picture plane or other homo-geneous field(s) in space.

Motion or gesture

Type and image are acted on by a common force, or affected by the implied motion of a human or mechanical gesture.

Metaphor

Type and image are fused by a calculated visual metaphor that operates through mutual dependency of the verbal and pictorial elements.

Applications

To blend two or more things that aren't customarily related to make a strong association between them

To strengthen an existing conceptual connection through harmony and integration in order to present a galvanized point of view, such as a political or poetic statement

To create an altered reality that challenges the viewer to reexamine a particular subject from an unexpected perspective

Fusion is one of the most ambitious ways to merge type and image. For fusion to be successful, the interrelationship between the type and image must be honest, coherent, and credible. Forming such a convincing alliance requires both imagination and ingenuity.

FUSION

In order to "wrap" the word *Chicago* around the existing building facades in the primary image for this poster for an exhibition on Chicago architecture, Philippe Apeloig patiently worked in his studio with large letterforms on cardboard. He set the letters at various angles until he achieved a logical optical viewpoint. Once the perfectly angled word was superimposed over the photograph, the type and image jelled and the poster was set in motion. The black word *Chicago* in forced perspective leaps off the surface of the sepia-toned historical photograph and underscores the emerging grandeur of the city at the turn of the last century. The black frame around the image acts as a threshold to another dimension, and visually reinforces the denotative presence of the matching black type. This extends the illusion ever so slightly and builds a poster space that surpasses the original photographic space.

Apeloig created large-scale mock-ups of the title type and photographed them at different camera angles. He then imposed the image of the type onto the photograph.

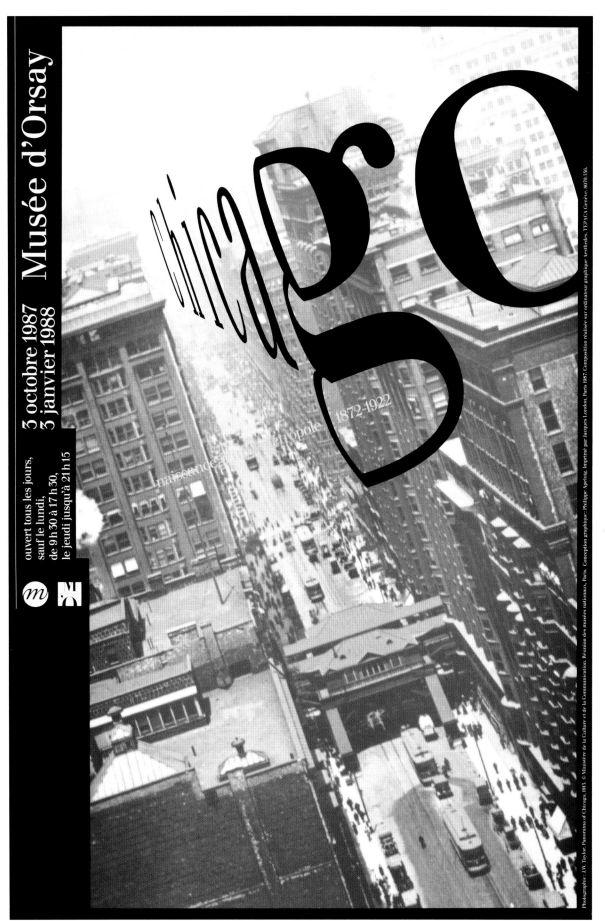

Musée d'Orsay

3 octobre 1987
3 janvier 1988

ouvert tous les jours,
sauf le lundi,
de 9 h 30 à 17 h 30,
le jeudi jusqu'à 21 h 15

chicago

naissance d'une métropole 1872-1922

Photographie : J.W. Taylor, Panorama of Chicago, 1913. © Ministère de la Culture et de la Communication, Réunion des musées nationaux, Paris. Conception graphique : Philippe Apeloig. Imprimé par Jacques London, Paris 1987. Composition réalisée sur ordinateur graphique Aesthedes, TEPACA Genève, 8070/356.

Philippe Apeloig's final
poster fuses type and
image into a sensational
depiction of Chicago
emerging as a preeminent
urban force at the turn of
the twentieth century.

PROJECT
*Poster: Chicago,
Birth of a Metropolis*
CLIENT
Musée d'Orsay
Paris, France
DESIGNER
Philippe Apeloig
Apeloig Design
Paris, France

This photograph by Lee Friedman was the initial inspiration for the poster.

With the use of single-point perspective, Jean-Benoît Lévy establishes a strong connection between the viewer and the message of this poster for a flea market in Aarberg, Switzerland. The interdependency of lines, type, and image forms a strong dynamic sense of space, which is enhanced by selectively focused (sharp and soft) typographic elements arranged in a radial formation around a woman's face. The text sits on the lines like objects caught in a web. Through these devices, Lévy captures the experience of attending the market, and "spotting" and "trapping" objects of personal value.

The primary title, *Puce,* is much larger than the secondary information; this discrepancy further activates the viewer's sense of involvement. Looking at these preliminary studies (below)—two of many explorations of radiating text—helps explicate Lévy's decision-making process.

PROJECT
Advertising poster for a flea market
CLIENT
**Organization Puce Aarberg
Aarberg, Switzerland**
DESIGNER
**Jean-Benoît Lévy
AND (Trafic Grafic)
Basel, Switzerland /
San Francisco, USA**
PHOTOGRAPHER
**Lee Friedman
San Francisco, USA**

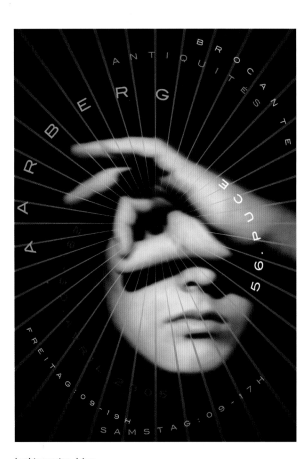

In this version, Lévy experimented with multicolored concentric circles of type.

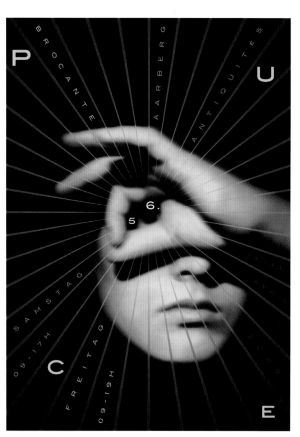

This is closer to the final design but without the type in perspective with the lines.

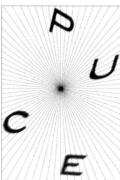

The diagrammatic rendering (above) reveals the analytical structure and symmetry of the underlying grid. The lines originate at the center point and are evenly spaced at five-degree angles.

In the final poster, Lévy optically distorted the type and placed it within the framework to convincingly fuse type and image. The poster's radial structure engages the viewer in a powerful invitation to shop at the Puce annual flea market.

FUSION

PROJECT
Poster for annual student architecture competition
CLIENT
Lyceum Fellowship Cambridge, Massachusetts, USA
DESIGNERS
Nancy Skolos and Thomas Wedell Skolos-Wedell Canton, Massachusetts, USA
PHOTOGRAPHER
Thomas Wedell Canton, Massachusetts, USA

The designers added white reflections in Adobe Photoshop to enhance the optical illusion and to fuse the magnifying glass with the poster frame.

The designers were charged with generating interest for this annual student architectural competition by shedding light on the subject without suggesting a definite solution for the assignment. The competition design problem was based on the premise that people see only small glimpses of the natural landscape but rarely experience the true vitality and fragility of the wilderness. Therefore students were asked to design intimate shelters to be sited in remote areas for contemplating the outdoors.

Observing and framing were the conceptual directives that began the creative process. The designers quickly came up with three fundamental components: images from nature, a human hand, and a lens. They sketched them into collages. Once the designers established a direction, they began the process of making the final image in the studio and completed it as a single "staged" studio setup. A photograph of a tree in a meadow, taken at dusk, was placed under the camera and surrounded by cardboard suspended above to outline a "window" around the photo. The magnifying glass, placed in front of the tree, became a symbol for observation.

In the final poster (opposite), the oversized white word *Lyceum* and number *2002* eclipsed by black undersized text boxes further manipulate the viewer's experience. The smaller type, used for jurors' names and prizes, appears to be reacting to the magnifying glass, migrating away in an arc. This begins to suggest *fragmentation,* something we will be discussing later.

Initial collage sketches were constructed from quick photos of a hand, a magnifying glass, and a landscape photo.

A strobe-lit landscape photo was the starting point for the design process. Photographer Thomas Wedell suspended the magnifying glass over the photographic print and then rephotographed the image for the poster.

To further suggest observation from inside a shelter, pieces of mat board were positioned above the photograph.

FUSION

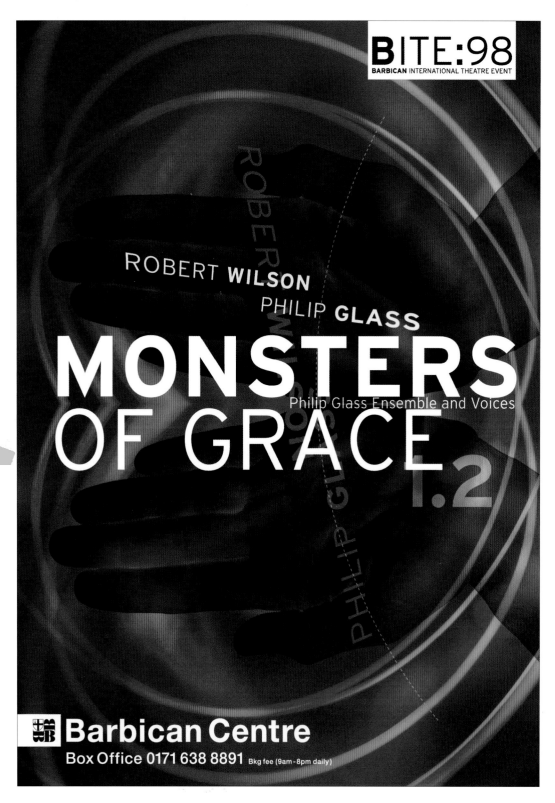

All three of these posters evoke an edgy, unsettling optical transformation. Distorted, transparent, X-ray-like images of human faces and hands, and provocative title type fuse under a high-tech membrane to create an altered reality.

The symmetrical mirroring in this poster represents the collaboration between composer Philip Glass and designer/director Robert Wilson for this stage production of *Monsters of Grace*. The hypnotic optical qualities—lateral symmetry, concentric radiating auras, and digitally processed colors—allude to the experimental media used in the actual stage performance.

Robert Wilson worked with a team of digital media designers to produce 70mm computer-animated images, which the audience viewed with 3D glasses. Philip Glass, whose repetitive compositional structures create a mesmerizing atmosphere, wrote the music. These two highly creative individuals' experimental production created an energetic alternate reality that the poster captured.

The director's and composer's names are superimposed on a pair of hands, communicating the dynamism of two creative forces coming together.

PROJECT
Poster: *Monsters of Grace*
CLIENT
Barbican Centre
London, UK
DESIGNER
Why Not Associates
London, UK

Type and image blend both visually and conceptually in this poster for an exhibition of communication and new media. A sphere is the prevailing force that fuses all the elements into a cohesive whole. Appearing much like a fish-eye lens, the surface of the poster engulfs the human face, the typography of the artists' names, and the texture of the video monitor. All elements are engaged and transformed within this globe-shaped picture plane, making a very strong statement about the current relationship between people and the media.

Peter Moser heads a team of ten at Velvet Creative Office. Collaboration, exchange of ideas, and interests in the world of media, architecture, fashion, and society inspire the studio's work. When asked about the type/image relationship, Peter Moser reflects, "There's no fixed rule.... It's probably the same as in every relationship: from perfect fusion to irritation, from hate to love—they simply have to be in a relation and not stand next to each other."

PROJECT
Poster for the exhibition "Ich & Du" (Me & You)
CLIENT
Museum für Gestaltung Zurich, Switzerland
DESIGNER
Peter Moser
Velvet Creative Office GmbH
Lucerne, Switzerland

The human becomes one with technology in this poster for an exhibition about communication and new media.

PROJECT
Poster for the exhibition "Frankensteins Kinder—Film und Medizin" (Frankenstein's Children—Film and Medicine)
CLIENT
Museum für Gestaltung Zurich, Switzerland
DESIGNER
Peter Moser
Velvet Creative Office GmbH
Lucerne, Switzerland

In this poster for the exhibition "Frankensteins Kinder—Film und Medizin" (Frankenstein's Children—Film and Medicine), type and image blend to conjure an ominous atmosphere of biological experimentation.

PROJECT
APICORP annual
report covers
CLIENT
APICORP (Arab Petroleum
Investment Corporation)
Dammen, Saudi Arabia
DESIGNER
Siobhan Keaney
London, UK

Sometimes the lens that fuses type, image, and message comes straight from the designer's eye and mind. These two report covers by Siobhan Keaney show her unique way of depicting contemporary issues of media, technology, and events. They are examples of how organic fusion can be used to merge many aspects of a subject into a unified statement.

Siobhan Keaney's solutions for the APICORP annual reports show an organic fusion of science and technology. In the illustration (above) light and motion fuse the type and image into an animated liquid surface, expressing the energy of Earth's natural resources. By isolating this "explosion" of motion against a darkened background, the designer has further enhanced the effectiveness of the message.

The cover (below) features Earth as a central, monumental object, a solid fixed presence within the composition. Swirling "clouds" formed from maps, light, and corporate logos in two languages frame the planet and fuse the composition into a combined poetic statement that strengthens the corporation's message concerning its connection to the world and its resources.

In these special-edition stamps commemorating English novelist H. G. Wells, the designer references vintage futuristic imagery and special effects—the vortex, aerodynamic forms, and saturated color—to create a small moment of fantasy. The designs take the viewer back to the future as it may have been depicted in the late nineteenth century. Like a miniature movie poster, each stamp condenses one of Wells's science fiction themes into a single snapshot that fuses text and image into a single cohesive message.

PROJECT
Science fiction special-edition stamps celebrating the centenary of *The Time Machine* by H.G. Wells
CLIENT
Royal Mail
London, UK
DESIGNER
Siobhan Keaney
London, UK

Royal Mail postage stamp designs commemorating the H.G. Wells centennial celebration in England. The designs place the viewer in a miniature imaginary space.

Clockwise from top: Space Travel/*The First Men in the Moon;* Alien Invasion/*The War of the Worlds;* Time Travel/ *The Time Machine;* Futuristic Society/*Things to Come.*

FUSION

In Ralph Schraivogel's work, form and content are developed simultaneously through a painstaking process of making and discovery. Working slowly with various visual phenomena, he molds an impression that gradually forms an integrated surface pattern. The picture plane becomes a unified singular effect; all the elements appear as if they were always meant to be together.

For his solution to a poster (left) for a flea market in Aarberg, a small town on the Aare river in Switzerland, Ralph Schraivogel fused the type onto a captivating watery surface. Letters spelling the name of the event, *Puce* (flea in French), are isolated in four circles that modulate the picture plane. The vortices are an abstract representation of fleas jumping in water that disrupt the informational text, and create a state of flux and fascination.

This poster (opposite), designed by Ralph Schraivogel for an exhibition of his own work, is really a self-portrait, not only of the designer himself, but also of his posters. The central image is the hand of the designer, breaking through and agitating the graphically dotted surface of the picture plane. The disruption has occurred, yet things are somehow still very coherent, defined meticulously by the order of the dots and the yellow strips of type (reminiscent of caution tape) that are still legible.

PROJECT
Poster for flea market
CLIENT
**Organization Puce Aarberg
Aarberg, Switzerland**
DESIGNER
**Ralph Schraivogel
Atelier Schraivogel
Zurich, Switzerland**

**Surface tension fuses with
text to provoke the viewer's
interest in an upcoming
street market in Switzerland.**

PROJECT
Poster for exhibition
of Ralph Schraivogel's
posters
CLIENT
Schule für Gestaltung
Bern, Switzerland
DESIGNER
Ralph Schraivogel
Atelier Schraivogel
Zurich, Switzerland

This poster for his one-
man exhibition clearly
exhibits Schraivolgel's
love of the picture plane.

FUSION

PROJECT
Poster for exhibition
CLIENT
**Museum für Gestaltung,
Zurich, Switzerland**
DESIGNER
**Ralph Schraivogel
Atelier Schraivogel
Zurich, Switzerland**

In this poster (left) for an exhibition of the work of Art Nouveau architect and designer Henry van de Velde, Schraivogel places one of van de Velde's chairs center stage and then riffs off it with a pattern of crazy undulating lines—a close-up of an optical moiré pattern—that surround the nineteenth-century artifact with a contemporary energy. The viewer gets lost in the network of optical phenomena and spacial alignments that are constantly occurring within the picture plane.

The merging of type and image was especially challenging in this case because the image was finished first. In order to make an integrated surface for the type, the designer repeated the moiré pattern of the background but straightened it to align with the blocks of text.

Schraivogel has been designing vibrant posters for the film festival Cinémafrica for many years. To make the zebralike patterns that energize this poster (opposite), he created Newton rings by using a vacuum to make air pockets between layers of acetate. He enlarged the results to fill this world-format poster (standard Swiss size: 50.4" × 35.6" [1,280 × 905 mm]) and silk-screened it on craft paper in white and black ink.

This high-contrast rendering of the poster shows how the type was imposed on the image. Strips of white were carved out of the image to preserve legibility in the small type.

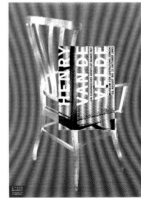

An organic pattern is fused with a highly rational text treatment in this active poster for a festival of African film.

PROJECT
Poster for film festival
CLIENT
Afrika-Filmtage/
Filmpodium
Zurich, Switzerland
DESIGNER
Ralph Schraivogel
Atelier Schraivogel
Zurich, Switzerland

In this poster (opposite), the type is embedded in an organdy ribbon that twists and turns in a labyrinth-like path from one edge of the picture plane to the other. The viewer's eye and mind take a visual journey that parallels the experience of listening to jazz. The wrapping and coiling create a buoyancy and resilience that capture the viewer's attention. The poster is a source of endless embellishment: not merely decorative, but a performance. The dominant visual theme displays continuous variations as its formal possibilities are played out.

Schraivogel has fused type and image together in a treatment (right) that resembles the mountainous terrain of the Swiss Alps in this unified visual metaphor, highlighting the acronym for the client's name (AGI). To get this effect, he simply placed a piece of crinkled aluminum foil on his photocopier and made copies at three different angles. The photocopies were then separated into three printing colors: black, gray, and silver.

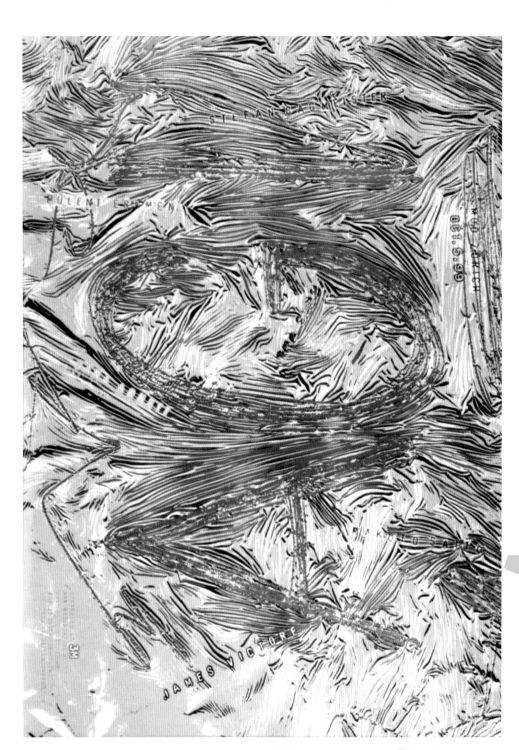

The designer fuses a ribbonlike structure with informational text to promote a jazz festival (opposite).

PROJECT
Poster for jazz festival
CLIENT
Jazzfestival
Schaffhausen, Switzerland
DESIGNER
Ralph Schraivogel
Atelier Schraivogel
Zurich, Switzerland

PROJECT
Poster for a graphic design seminar
CLIENT
Alliance Graphique Internationale Congress Pontresina, Switzerland
DESIGNER
Ralph Schraivogel
Atelier Schraivogel
Zurich, Switzerland

This poster, commemorating a seminar for Alliance Graphique Internationale in Pontresina, Switzerland, resembles an aerial view of the Alps. It is an extraordinary example of the fusion of surface and message.

Detail of Sporen poster
reveals a highly complex
optical surface.

PROJECT
Poster for a dance and
music concert
CLIENT
Leine Roebana
DESIGNER
Alvin Chan
Koeweiden Postma
PHOTOGRAPHER
Deen van Meer
Amsterdam, Netherlands

This poster is a vivid
example of the use of
scale change to reveal
different meanings at
various viewing distances.

A horizontal matrix, articulated by dots and dingbats, expresses the music of Sporen. Because the word *sporen* means to travel by rail, some of the selected icons reinforce the travel theme by depicting various destinations—campgrounds, desert with cactus, cruise ship, and beach with umbrella. There are also whimsical and nonsensical symbols mixed in: speech bubbles, hardware, tools, and various punctuation marks. The poster plays with the viewer's perception by revealing details gradually from various viewing distances. From far away only the word *Sporen* and a vague image of a walking figure are discernible. As the viewer moves a bit closer, the careful alignment of dots, lines, and letterspaced type becomes increasingly evident. The musicians' names are also quite legible, with line spacing that fits the grid. At even closer range, the viewer discovers smaller type messages and icons.

Poster detail shows
enlarged grain structure
within the image.

The use of coarse, high-contrast black and white film grain and pixels
renders this archetypal battle scene—of soldiers in combat against an
exploding sky, with military aircraft flying overhead. The relentlessness
of the war machine is emphasized by the repetition in the surface pattern
and the bitmapped, monospaced typography. Even the airplanes appear to
have been multiplied as a step-and-repeat pattern. Against the darkened
background, the designers have highlighted a few words and human
figures in white, to provide a trace of hope in an otherwise desolate scene
of conflict and destruction

PROJECT
Antiwar poster
CLIENT
Kampagne gegen
Wehrpflicht,
Zwangsdienste und
Militär (Campaign Against
Selective Service, Forced
Labor and Military)
DESIGNER/
PHOTOGRAPHER
cyan
Berlin, Germany

A gritty panorama in this
antiwar poster carries the
message "Jeder hat jeden
tag die Möglichkeit, sich
zu verweigern" (Each day
brings everyone the
opportunity to refuse).

PROJECT
Calendar typomoon
CLIENT
Self
DESIGNERS
Dieter Feseke
grappa dor/umbra-dor
Berlin, Germany

Red and black stripes containing the words of a song by Patti Smith create an inescapable rhythm on this calendar page.

PROJECT
Calendar typomoon
CLIENT
Self
Berlin, Germany
DESIGNER
Dieter Feseke,
Frank Döring, and
Kerstin Baarmann
grappa dor/umbra-dor
Berlin, Germany

Electric green dots and dashes layered over a soft-focus portrait of an Aborigine reference Morse code on this calendar page for Typomoon.

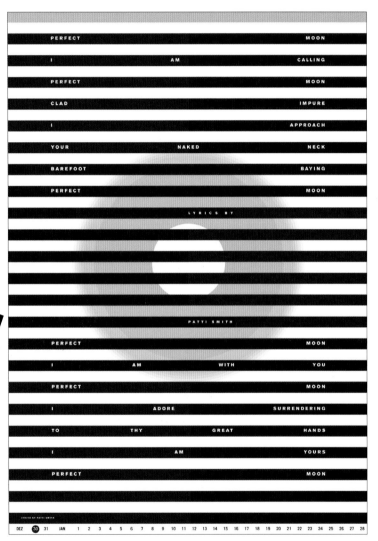

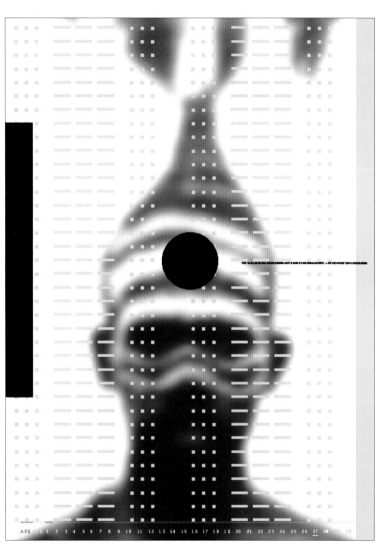

Horizontal banding fuses the surface of these calendar pages created for a self-promotion calendar called Typomoon, an annual calendar honoring prominent people in architecture, art, music, sports, or the sciences. The only consistent visual requirement, a circle, represents the phases of the moon within the picture plane.

In the first calendar page, the words from a song titled "Perfect Moon" by Patti Smith are spread across the picture plane onto bands that resemble window blinds. The "moon," depicted as a soft circle, appears to be glowing from behind these sharp-edged slats.

The second example features telegraph inventor Samuel F. B. Morse's system of dots and dashes, which served as the inspiration for the design. The pattern of three dots, three dashes, three dots is the code for *SOS*. When the code is enlarged, the big dot illustrates the full moon.

Type spelling the word
terts ("thirds") is fused
into the surface of this
composition, creating an
organic effect.

PROJECT
**Poster: *Terts* (Thirds)
dance poster**
CLIENT
**Leine Roebana
Amsterdam,
Netherlands**
DESIGNER
**Brian Hoffer
Koeweiden Postma
Amsterdam,
Netherlands**

In this poster the word *terts,* which is Dutch for *thirds,* and refers to the musical interval "thirds," is embossed into the surface. For Jacques Koeweiden, the designer, more often than not "the type and/or image are the result of a series of solutions that come straight from the concept." He is always open to any outcome that will provide the best solution for the problem. "Type in combination with image should make a *pas de deux,* where the viewer sees or feels a true relationship between the message,

image and text." In addition Koeweiden states that according to the art historian John Berger, "There are no photographs which can be denied, all photographs have the status of fact. What is to be examined is in what way photography can and cannot give meaning to facts." By imbedding the type into the photographic image, the designer has presented as fact the subject for the upcoming experimental dance program.

Type and image are fused and take motion within this lively poster designed for a theatrical production based on the Wenedikt Jerofejew novel, *Die Reise nach Petuschki* (Voyage to Petuschki), a story about a philanderer who gets progressively more inebriated as he travels from Moscow to visit his girlfriend in a Russian village.

The overall effect is a whimsical coalescence of the type and image merging together at what appears to be very high speed. The X shape could be a railroad-crossing sign seen along the journey, but it also resembles a human figure; possibly the woman the main character is seeking. The idea of a voyage is reinforced by the blurring of the image—the drunken protagonist's view out the window of a moving train.

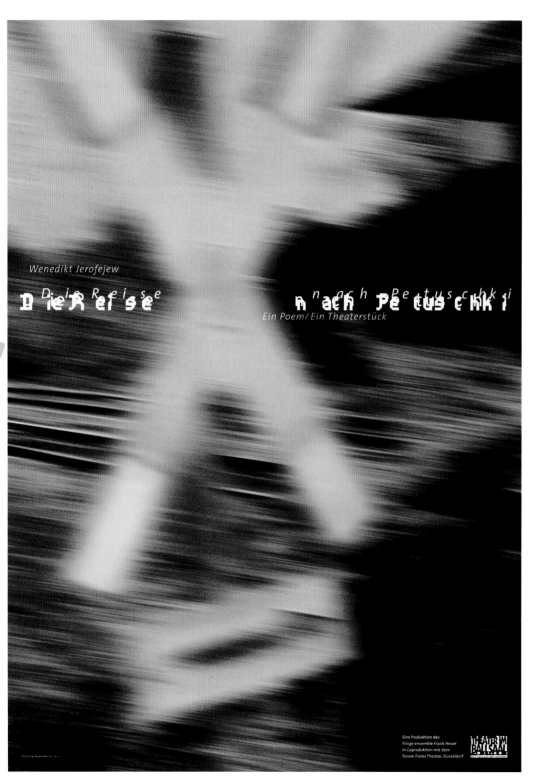

The dizzying image of this poster for a stage performance reflects the protagonist's state of mind as he gets progressively more inebriated. He dies from drunkenness at the end of the story.

PROJECT
Theater poster
CLIENT
Theater im Ballsaal
Bonn, Germany
DESIGNER
Heribert Birnbach
Birnbach Design
Bonn, Germany

The words *nicht grübeln* ("don't bother") seem to emerge from within the image of a stone traffic barrier in this poster for a cultural festival in Bonn, Germany.

Thomas Mann als Inspiration

Ein künstlerisches Projekt in der Thomas-Mann-Straße

4. bis 11. Oktober 1996

Informationen: Kunst Forum Bonn, Thomas-Mann-Straße 36   0228. 63 39 58

PROJECT
Poster for cultural festival
CLIENT
**Kunst Forum Bonn
Bonn, Germany**
DESIGNER
**Heribert Birnbach
Birnbach Design
Bonn, Germany**

In this poster the headline, *"Nicht grübeln!"* ("Don't bother!"), a quotation from Thomas Mann, makes an amusing fusion of word and image as it "collides" with a stone post in a photograph taken on the Thomas Mann Street in Bonn, where the festival takes place. The stone traffic barrier was frequently hit by passing cars. No one could understand why the stone wasn't removed because it did so much damage, scratching vehicles and heightening frustrations. The designer has used this image as a symbol, representing both the spirit and location of the street festival.

In this poster for an exhibition of the designer's photographs of cities, the text block emerges subtly and begins to appear as another element in the image.

PROJECT
Poster for Melk Imboden exhibition
CLIENT
Kornschütte Luzern Lucerne, Switzerland
DESIGNER/
PHOTOGRAPHER
Melchior Imboden Bouchs, Switzerland

Time passing is the subject expressed in both the photo and typography of this poster (opposite) for *Zeitbilder* (Time Pictures), an exhibition of large-format photographs taken of big cities by Melchior Imboden over twenty years.

The photograph in this poster is of Manhattan, shot from an elevated position with an extended time exposure. This technique caused extensive blurring of the city's lights and produced multiple V-shaped bursts that descend vertically on the surface of the picture plane. The type blends with the photograph; in the same blue and black tones, and is set in a typeface that relates to the angular shape of the light forms. The synthesis is completed by the orientation of the titling information, which runs vertically up the side of the poster. Its flush-left, ragged-right format creates an outline that mimics the stepped back profiles of the skyscrapers.

Motion is again the force that fuses elements together in this poster (below) for an exhibition of the video art of Irene Naef, who was invited to reinterpret, and make new art forms from, the costumes and fashion design collection of the Nidwaldner Museum.

The poster uses a still image from one of Naef's videos of clothes in a washing machine. The swirling of the fabric, reflections in the glass door of the washer, and water droplets envelop the surface of the poster and resemble the visual effects in the "Zeitbilder" poster (opposite). Color and motion blend with the image, and the type lands firmly and legibly at the top of the poster to suspend the energy without completely breaking it. While the use of motion is similar, the resulting emotion is quite different. In "Zeitbilder" the viewer absorbs the contemplative solitude of the photograph, but in this poster there is the feeling of a performance, with energy much like dance, theater, or carnival.

For a poster announcing a video presentation by the artist Irene Naef, the designer has chosen one frame from her interpretive imagery, and has fused the text information into its surface.

PROJECT
Poster for exhibition:
"In Hülle und Fülle"
(In covering [or holes]
and abundance)
CLIENT
Nidwaldner Museum
Stans, Switzerland
DESIGNER
Melchior Imboden
Bouchs, Switzerland
PHOTOGRAPHER
Irene Naef
Lucerne, Switzerland

FUSION

PROJECT
Poster: *Im Fluss*
CLIENT
Musical Event on
the Rhine River
DESIGNER
Jean-Benoît Lévy
AND (Trafic Grafic)
Basel, Switzerland/
San Francisco, USA
PHOTOGRAPHER
Daniel Furon
San Francisco, USA

To create a poster advertising a summer concert on the Rhine River in Switzerland, Jean-Benoît Lévy worked to connect the theme of music with the feeling and meaning of water. Lévy's keen eye and imagination have taught him not to rely on his memory of something, not even something as familiar as water. Through the process of designing, one must discover the subject as if for the first time and relay that sense of discovery to the viewer.

The physical qualities of water, its patterns, movement, reflections, and colors are closely examined in a series of photographic studies. (below, top row)

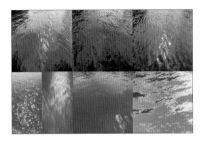

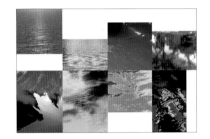

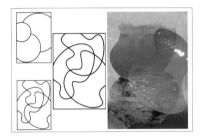

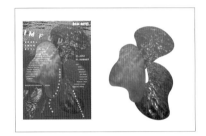

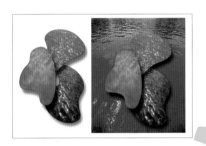

Lévy translated the qualities of water into form in these sketches. The forms take the shape of rocks, waves, and painting palettes. (above, bottom row)

The posters have a strong impact on the street. The flat, upright planes of color introduce the feeling of water into the urban landscape.

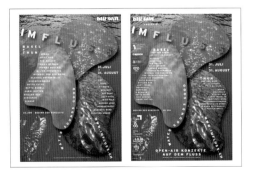

Lévy placed the words *water sounds good* and the names of the performers and kinds of music on the waveforms to flow on the page.

In his monograph/novel *A Guide to Ecstacity,* London architect Nigel Coates interlaces impressions of seven cities from around the world—Cairo, London, Mumbai, New York, Rio, Rome, and Tokyo. Chapter headings—"Tuning in," "Looking on," "Undressing," "Letting go," "Cranking up," and "Flipping out"—invite the reader to participate in, not just examine from a distance, the dynamics of urban city space and mind space. The intricate design renders these points of view in dreamy panoramic spreads, where the type and photography commingle to form a lively reality.

PROJECT
Book: *Guide to Ecstacity*
CLIENT
Nigel Coates
London, UK
DESIGN
Why Not Associates
London, UK

FUSION

Lively typographic composition sets the stage on the cover of this graphically experimental guide by Nigel Coates.

Photographs fuse into graphic shapes and text blocks move seamlessly across the page, creating the sense of a city in motion.

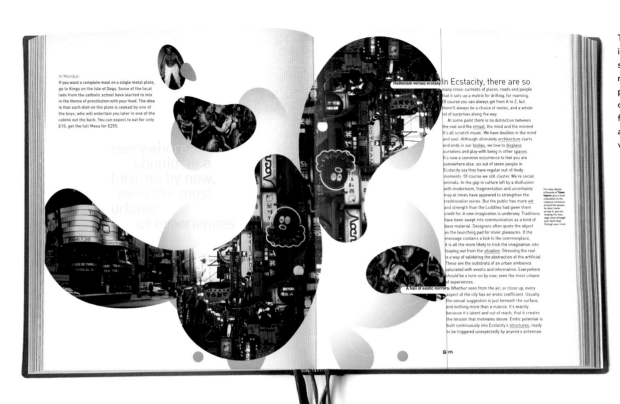

In Mumbai:
If you want a complete meal on a single metal plate, go to Kings on the Isle of Dogs. Some of the local lads from the catholic school have started to mix in the theme of prostitution with your food. The idea is that each dish on the plate is cooked by one of the boys, who will entertain you later in one of the cabins out back. You can expect to eat for only E10, get the full Mesa for E255.

*everywhere
should be a
turn-on by now,
even the most
urbane
of experiences*

Hedonism versus ecstasy: In Ecstacity, there are so many cross-currents of places, roads and people that it sets up a matrix for drifting, for roaming. Of course you can always get from A to Z, but there'll always be a choice of routes, and a whole lot of surprises along the way.

At some point there is no distinction between the real and the virtual, the mind and the minded. It's all scratch music. We have doubles in the mind and soul. Although ultimately architecture starts and ends in our bodies, we love to displace ourselves and play with being in other spaces. It's now a common occurrence to feel you are somewhere else: six out of seven people in Ecstacity say they have regular out-of-body moments. Of course we still cluster. We're social animals. In the gap in culture left by a disillusion with modernism, fragmentation and uncertainty may at times have appeared to strengthen the traditionalist voices. But the public has more wit and strength than the Luddites had given them credit for. A new imagination is underway. Traditions have been swept into communication as a kind of base material. Designers often quote the abject as the launching pad for ironic pleasures. If the message contains a link to the commonplace, it is all the more likely to trick the imagination into leaping out from the situation. Stressing the real is a way of validating the abstraction of the artificial. These are the substrata of an urban ambience saturated with events and information. Everywhere should be a turn-on by now, even the most urbane of experiences.

A hall of exotic mirrors: Whether seen from the air, or close up, every aspect of the city has an erotic coefficient. Usually the sexual suggestion is just beneath the surface, and nothing more than a nuance. But that's exactly because it's latent and out of reach, that it creates the tension that motivates desire. Erotic potential is built continuously into Ecstacity's structures, ready to be triggered unexpectedly by anyone's antennae.

The waxy digital billboards of Times Square give a fixed undulation to the corporeal enclosure around the square. As data tracks across it, you are reading the message more through your flesh than through your mind.

395

The city scenes packed into these amorphous shapes create a macro-micro view. The reader's perception of the activity on this urban street shifts from a great distance to an up-close, personalized viewpoint.

Server. The most revived contemporary art and architecture in Ecstacity exert, and a way to her own reading of Ecstacity and thus following of architecture space sets up more spaces, would you would go through? In the city one you are of different architectures work to serve as examples of pleasure. You would get through a much more attached to your experience of a tamper curves, your city. Which is money... continue around, then Ecstacity, each of a... again as it communicates you.

...up, match. This place seems to go beyond the usual commercial libido. It responds and reacts.

Old transportation forms, such as the metro and the rail system, which have been radically improved by magnetic lift, and the S-tram network, helps link local destinations with ease and shorter journey times. Both represent speed and value compared with easyCabs, but if you need to arrive superfast, then take an air-taxi. If your destination is east of Canary Wharf in Cairo-central, river taxis cut down journey times considerably. Rickshaws are slow, but you get the best view by being in the thick of things. Motorbikes have the best reach (and cut through restricted traffic zones), especially when using their own special elevated routes slung below the magnetic rails that cross-lace the city an average of six storeys up. Get the story in any of seven languages on tourist buses and bateaux-mouches. Get the view of the whole of Ecstacity from the Giant's Eye. Virgin's Airshopping Malls lift off hourly from terminals in each of the seven zones. Book or hire on www.ecstacity.com/getabout.

Then there's body power: skating, cycling, riding, biking, walking, running, strolling: change your speed in Ecstacity. Try moving at a new pace. As you gear-shift through your sensory mechanisms, different speeds tune you into different things. Catch a glimpse of the tops of buildings or a nice pair of legs.

Figure out where you're going. Choose a destination from the following pages: the best market for your taste and pocket, the best local deli, the best supermarket for late-night stockpiling (and/or cruising); the best open dinner parties. Find arenas to practise your sport, and take time off at the most testing of clubs and bars. Find your path by taking to the streets yourself. Remember that in Ecstacity nothing turns out as it seemed it would.

Poking around: Stick your nose into things. Ask how much. Take the time to check out local information sources that supplement the Internet. Newsstands are key trading posts in the city, exploiting the fact that they

The Aprilia motorbike by industrial designers Seymour Powell takes the artist to an extreme. Although an supplicating mode, this bike's hands body will help you do the ton.

VITESSE

131

Set against a dramatic black background, the images and type "dance" in this elegant invitation for an interdisciplinary theater class at the Bauhaus. The interaction is suggestive of the artist Wassily Kandinsky's work and his ideas about visual structure. Reminiscent of *Point and Line to Plane,* Kandinsky's seminal work on composition, the spaced letters make words and lines that direct the eye of the viewer through the poster space. The engraved diagrams of the human anatomy by Bauhaus teacher Oskar Schlemmer act as a mediating device between the photograph and the typography. The overall effect is a seamless merger of type, image, and message.

FUSION

The gestures in this invitation fuse through the integration of images (both drawn and photographed), graphic line work, and well considered type placement.

PROJECT
Invitation to theater class
CLIENT
**Bauhaus Dessau
Foundation
Dessau, Germany**
DESIGNERS
**Detlef Fiedler and
Daniela Haufe
cyan
Berlin, Germany**
PHOTOGRAPHER
Erich Consemüller
DRAWING
Oskar Schlemmer

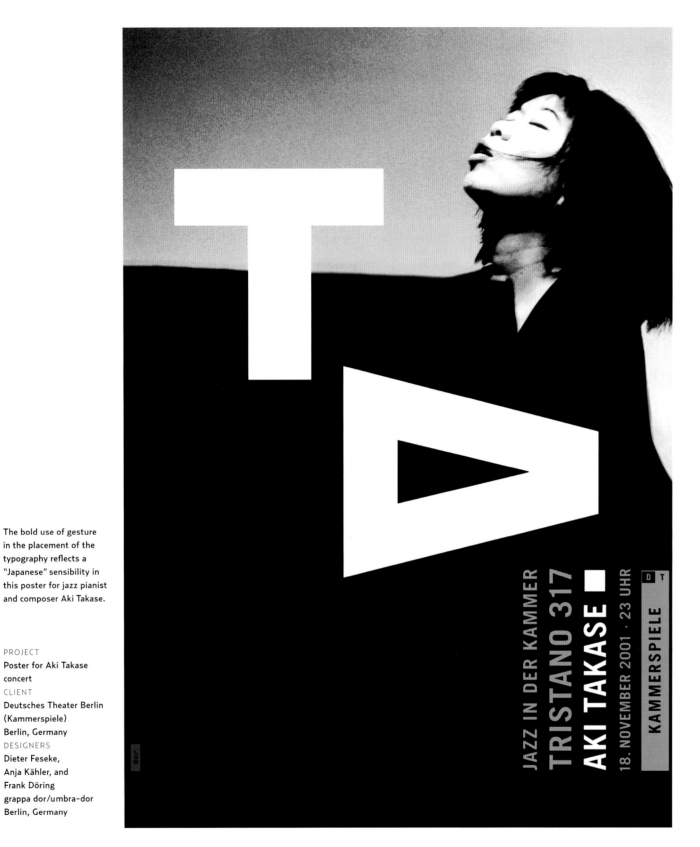

The bold use of gesture in the placement of the typography reflects a "Japanese" sensibility in this poster for jazz pianist and composer Aki Takase.

PROJECT
Poster for Aki Takase concert
CLIENT
Deutsches Theater Berlin (Kammerspiele)
Berlin, Germany
DESIGNERS
Dieter Feseke,
Anja Kähler, and
Frank Döring
grappa dor/umbra-dor
Berlin, Germany

The type and image meet halfway in this sublime poster for Japanese jazz pianist and composer Aki Takase. The language of the type and image are completely synchronized: both are bold yet meditative. There is a sense of mastery and "Japanese" sensibility in the decisive placement of each element. Nearly three-quarters of the image is an expanse of black space, filled by the viewer's imagination—it might be the performer's costume, or it might be a piano. Aki Takase's expressive face in the upper right corner begins a gesture that is completed by the large simplified letterforms of her initials, which intersect her body like the sleeves of a kimono.

R2 design of Portugal has successfully fused type with image in these two theatrical posters, where the words literally speak forth from the picture plane. In both there is a beauty in the photograph itself, its composition and cropping, but it is the typography's animated presence on the page that makes these posters so extraordinary.

The designers enjoy creating a dialogue between words and pictures and connecting those elements: In the *Molly Bloom* poster there is a relationship between the surface, the image, and the text. The name *Molly Bloom* emerges from the mouth of the woman, creating a conceptual and visual relationship between the image and type. The letters merge and become an active part of the image—but still maintain some distinction, appearing in red over the black and white photograph.

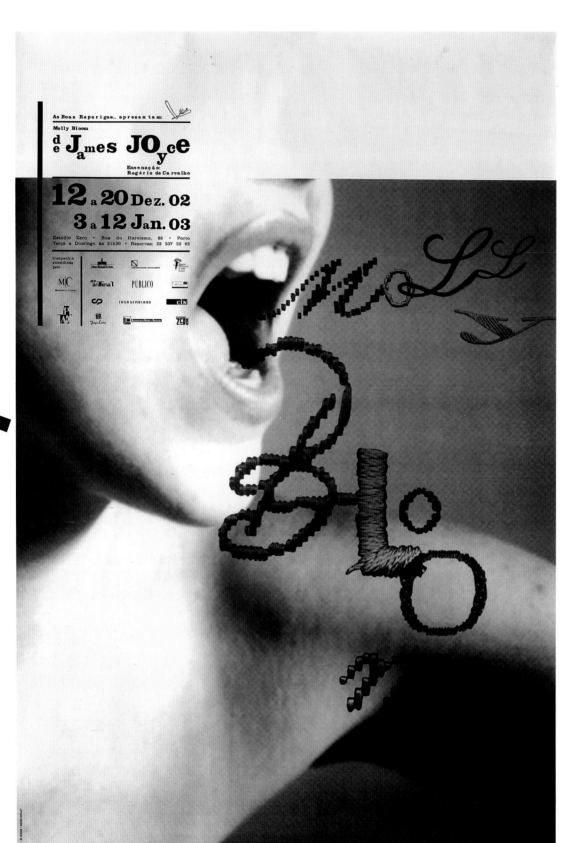

A collection of letters taken from embroidery on clothing is collaged to express the passion of words in this poster for a play inspired by the character Molly Bloom in James Joyce's *Ulysses*.

PROJECT
Poster: *Molly Bloom*
CLIENT
As Boas Raparigas
Porto, Portugal
DESIGNERS
Lizà Ramalho, Artur Rebelo, and Nadine Ouellet
R2 Design
Matosinhos, Portugal
PHOTOGRAPHERS
Lizà Ramalho and Nadine Ouellet

In fact, it is the crude quality of the red words spun like yarn against the elegant photograph that captures the essence of Molly Bloom's character. Her famous soliloquy from the end of James Joyce's *Ulysses* inspired this theatrical production:

I was a Flower of the mountain yes when I put the rose in my hair like the Andalusian girls used or shall I wear a red yes and how he kissed me under the Moorish wall and I thought well as well him as another and then I asked him with my eyes to ask again yes and then he asked me would I yes to say yes my mountain flower and first I put my arms around him yes and drew him down to me so he could feel my breasts all perfume yes and his heart was going like mad and yes I said yes I will yes.

The Boca poster (below), designed two years later in 2004, is an even more condensed snapshot of a narrative. The gesture, the word *boca* (mouth), is fused as tenderly as a kiss onto the page.

An extreme close-up of a kissing couple is used as a dramatic symbol for this poster for the stage play *Boca* (Mouth).

PROJECT
Poster: *Boca*
CLIENT
Teatro Bruto
DESIGNER
Lizá Ramalho and Artur Rebelo
R2 Design
Matosinhos, Portugal
PHOTOGRAPHER
Marco Mauriclo

Pierre Bernard has long valued human mark making—handwriting, pen-and-ink drawing, and traces of human contact—as a signifiers of moral truth, recognizing that people don't lie when they write something with their own hand. In his poster for an international design congress presented by Icograda (International Council of Graphic Design Associations) in Glasgow, Scotland, the designer has condensed the subject of an international forum for the exchange of new ideas into a photograph of a small globe, perhaps made of modeling clay (or a kneaded eraser), nestled into the palm of a hand. The informational text, written in ink on the hand, also contributes to the idea of human interaction. The globe appears to be leaving ink smudges on the hand, some discernible as continents, others only random expressive marks.

The power of this poster is in the dramatic contrast of the scale of the hand, the earth, and the handwritten text. The hand has opened to reveal the world inside; with this gesture, it asserts the values of a worldwide congress.

PROJECT
Poster for Design Renaissance Conference
CLIENT
Icograda Montreal, Canada
DESIGNER
Pierre Bernard Atelier de Création Graphique Paris, France

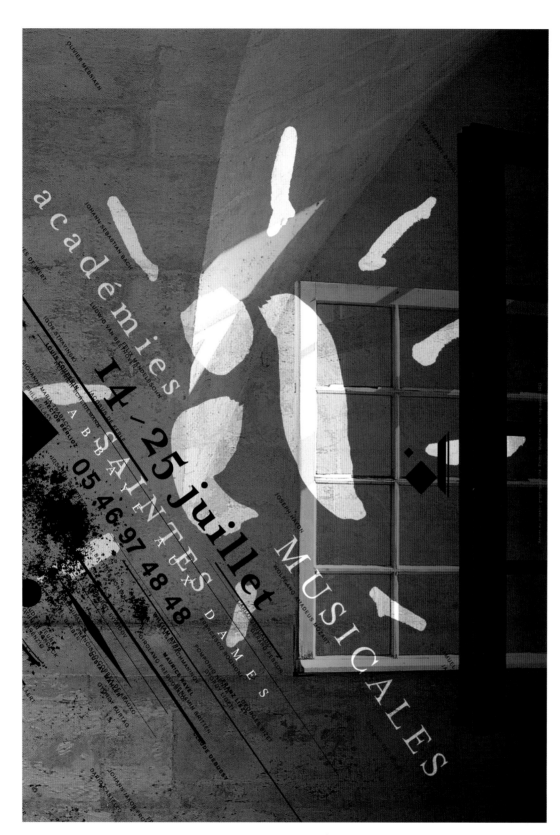

In this poster for a festival of sacred music in a small town in southwestern France, Bernard used spiritual symbols. The glowing hand-painted angel appears as if it is flying out of the open windows along with lines and bars of music, and the names of composers.

When asked about his process with type and image, Bernard said: *I try to start with a concept, generally weak and uncertain. I usually attempt to enter using one of the two entrances, image or type. If the concept is good and the context clear, the type and image (in a good design), make one. I don't like it when you need to trust the type first before being interested by the visual proposal. For me, type is only confirming what the image is offering to your intelligence and sensitivity. The type makes you sure of what you have grabbed in the image.*

PROJECT
Poster for music festival
CLIENT
Académies Musicales
Saintes
Saintes, France
DESIGNER
Pierre Bernard
Atelier de Création
Graphique
Paris, France

This poster for a concert of sacred music achieves its success by fusing together an unusual combination of illustration, photographic imagery, and text.

FUSION

Concept drives this poster for the opera *Carmen* through the successful fusion of symbolic typography and allegorical image.

PROJECT
Poster: *Carmen*
CLIENT
Badisches Staatstheatre
Karlsruhe, Germany
DESIGNER
Gunter Rambow
Rambow + van de Sand
Güstrow, Germany

This poster recalls the German PEN chapter's expulsion of writers the Nazi regime considered "undesirable."

PROJECT
Poster for exhibition:
"P.E.N. im Exil"
(P.E.N. in Exile)
CLIENT
Deutsche Bibliothek
Frankfurt am Main,
Germany
DESIGNER
Gunter Rambow
Rambow, Lienemeyer,
van de Sand
Güstrow, Germany

The fusion in this poster (opposite) is in the way the type and image bond to form a metaphor for the subject. The typographic necklace, placed at the top of an empty red dress, completes the portrait of Carmen, the flamboyant heroine of the opera. The dress, lying in torn pieces, symbolizes her death. The image is fused with the text in the viewer's mind to complete the meaning of the poster.

The way that the type and image partner to complete the story of Carmen is what makes the fusion so powerful. The type takes on a pictorial role to become part of the picture, making this poster have characteristics of inversion, a design technique covered in the fourth section of this book.

PEN, a worldwide association of writers, was formed in the years following World War I. The poster (above) promotes an exhibition titled "P.E.N. im Exil" (P.E.N. in Exile), focusing on Communist and Jewish writers that the German chapter of the organization expelled during the Nazi era.

The poster creates a powerful statement, capturing a moment in time when political bonds were often stronger than intellectual ones. The broken pencils make the swastika appear as an even more destructive force to the creative spirit. Again, fusion is operating on a more conceptual level, combining the text and image within the viewer's mind in order to fully express the emotions being represented within the finished work.

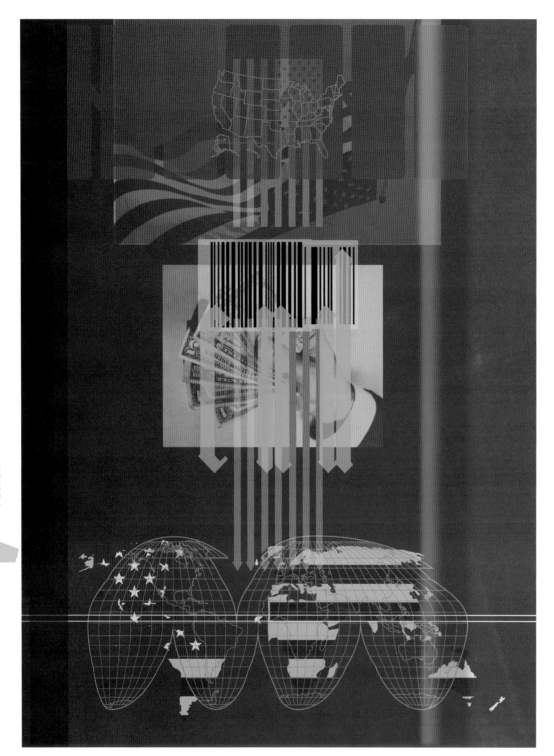

PROJECT
End of the World
billboard series
CLIENT
British Council
London, UK
DESIGNER
Jonathan Barnbrook
Barnbrook Design
London, UK

Multiple frames layered
within the picture plane
play against the sym-
metrical arrangement of
the images and text to
activate the space and
emphasize the subject:
the consumption of
resources.

Juxtaposed images of
hope and fear are depicted
in this final frame of
the series.

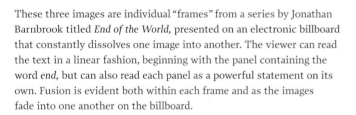

These three images are individual "frames" from a series by Jonathan Barnbrook titled *End of the World*, presented on an electronic billboard that constantly dissolves one image into another. The viewer can read the text in a linear fashion, beginning with the panel containing the word *end*, but can also read each panel as a powerful statement on its own. Fusion is evident both within each frame and as the images fade into one another on the billboard.

A strong vertical movement throughout the poster is created from stripes from the American flag, a bar code, and arrows pointing downward. The single word *end* appears in a super-condensed Gothic script that blends with the vertical elements.

PROJECT
Poster: *Violence Is
a Cycle 2004*
CLIENT
Self
DESIGNER
**Jonathan Barnbrook
Barnbrook Design
London, UK**

**The never-ending cycle
of violence is skillfully
depicted in this poster
designed to call attention
to the futility of killing.**

Jonathan Barnbrook's studio self-publishes antiwar and anti-advertising posters as part of its mission. This piece, illustrating the futility of killing, is an example of the studio's dedication to that philosophy.

The poster (above) features an outline map of Israel watched over by a laughing Yasser Arafat and smiling/clapping Ariel Sharon. There is an animated sense to both the type and the image: the circles are like wheels, and the diagonals are like the spokes of a wheel, making the viewer sense spinning and rotation and emphasizing the message of never-ending conflict. The exclamation marks also act as barriers at the corners of the composition to direct the viewer's eye back to the center.

1967   בכיה לדורות   2002

35 שנות כיבוש

35 YEARS OF OCCUPATION

With a strong social consciousness, David Tartakover initiates self-published posters to call attention to important issues affecting Israeli society. This poster is no exception. The designer successfully mixes collage with the use of strong gestured typography. From over the serrated horizon line appear miltary forces; below the horizon line soldiers stand at the ready. Large roman numeral XXXV representing thirty-five years of Israeli occupation of the Palestinian territories, advance vertically through the middle of the comp-osition. Additional text is placed horizontally, like signs nailed to a directional post, declaring a milestone or indicating a wrong direction.

At first the poster appears to be divided into three vertical columns, defined by the military figures. But a secondary structure soon makes itself apparent, through a combination of the zigzag horizon line and the black band containing text information that divides the poster horizontally into thirds. The intersection of these two systems creates an extremely dynamic composition.

PROJECT
Poster: *Thirty-Five Years of Occupation* 2002
CLIENT
Self
DESIGNER
David Tartakover
Tartakover Design
Tel Aviv, Israel
PHOTOGRAPHER
David Rubinger
Tel Aviv, Israel

Strong compositional elements reinforce the powerful message of this poster that commemorates the thirty-fifth year of occupation of the Palestinian territories by Israeli troops.

PROJECT
Poster: *Agadati*
CLIENT
Inbal Dance Company
Tel Aviv, Israel
DESIGNER
David Tartakover
Tartakover Design
Tel Aviv, Israel

This poster for the Israeli dance company Inbal fuses carefully calculated angular text with the softened image of a dancer to create a highly active and dramatic composition.

The Inbal Dance Company of Tel Aviv has established one of the foremost dance organizations in the world, mixing folklore, ethnic culture, biblical themes, and modern dance to depict the conflicts between modernity and tradition in Israeli culture.

David Tartakover has illustrated the mission of the dance company perfectly in this poster. The figure depicted is Baruch Agadati, one of the pioneers of modern dance in the 1920s.

The fusion of text and image creates a dynamic sense of motion, with flashes of color, contrasting angular forms, and gestural text. The grainy image of a traditional dancer appears ghostlike in soft gray against the stark red background, creating a sense of stage presence and has heightened the energy of the entire piece.

The dances are performed with organized well-calculated movements. In keeping with this tradition, the designer has been very meticulous in his placement of the text, emulating this sense of deliberate motion.

A typographic *0* is rendered in perspective with an angled "pop-up;" a shadow below it makes it connect with the image.

FUSION

This poster for Lyceum 2004 illustrates a design problem called "mending the landscape." The poster itself appears to have ruptured, revealing images beneath that correspond to features of the coastline—beach at the top, grasslands (rotated vertically) in the middle. The image comprises many materials, textures, and patterns, and they inform the way the type elements join with the picture plane

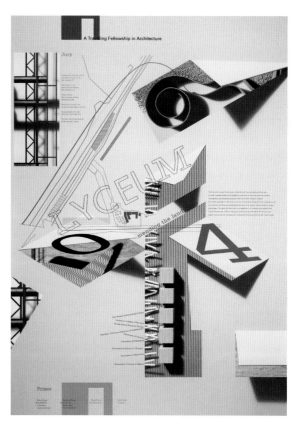

PROJECT
Poster for annual student architecture competition
CLIENT
Lyceum Fellowship Cambridge, Massachusetts, USA
DESIGNERS
Nancy Skolos and Thomas Wedell
Skolos-Wedell
Canton, Massachusetts, USA
PHOTOGRAPHER
Thomas Wedell
Canton, Massachusetts, USA

Openings in this poster's picture plane reveal abstracted compositions based on the actual site conditions for this student architecture competition.

The Boston Architectural Center
California College of the Arts
Rhode Island School of Design
Southern California Institute of Architecture
University of Arizona
University of Cincinnati
University of Illinois at Chicago
University of Minnesota
University of Hawaii at Manoa

The names of the participating schools are continued on lines suggested by the linear photographic elements.

PROJECT
Poster for annual student architecture competition
CLIENT
Lyceum Fellowship Cambridge, Massachusetts
DESIGNER
Nancy Skolos and Thomas Wedell Skolos-Wedell Canton, Massachusetts, USA
PHOTOGRAPHER
Thomas Wedell Canton, Massachusetts, USA

Detail showing the intersection of the type and artwork.

Motion and modularity are blended with nostalgic graphic elements in this poster for the 2003 Lyceum competition.

The Lyceum 2003 competition program challenged the students to reinvent the house on wheels. To reinforce this theme, the two zeros of the date were transformed into rounded "wheels." The designers then blended the completed date onto the photograph of the architectural model elements by overprinting red stripes adapted from house trailer graphics of the 1950s.

FRAGMENTATION

Type and image displace each other

Fragmentation occurs when type and image disturb or disrupt one another, usually with one providing the impetus for activating the state of flux. Designs in this category are often indexical, existing as evidence of either a past, present, or future interaction. Because of the unsettled nature of a design with fragmentation, the interrelationships have the potential for interweaving multiple meanings and sometimes require a high degree of decoding.

In fusion, motion is a unifying catalyst, but in fragmentation the elements are not evenly acted upon. While the force of fusion is to homogenize, the action of fragmentation is less predictable, much like a weather pattern.

Formal qualities

Irregularities

Elements are torn, divided, or unevenly dispersed.

Displacement

The composition appears as an individual frame that has been extracted from an animated film so that the type and image are frozen in their interaction.

Interruption

The type or image intrude on one another to punctuate or disconnect the message.

Exaggeration

Actions are amplified through scale, color, and complication.

Applications

Applications for fragmentation range across a broad spectrum. At one end, type and image are not quite synchronized but still work together to emphasize the friction between two or more ideas. At the other end, type and image form a high level of destabilization, resulting in a more active reading.

To animate and energize a message

To imply the passing of time or create a state of flux

To construct a complex message with multiple meanings

To create a surreal scenario with unpredictable results

To privilege one idea over another

To promote a play by the Israeli poet and writer Yitzchak Laor, designer David Tartakover has constructed a fragmented sequence of images and typographic gestures to reveal the jarring transition of one young Israeli citizen from civilian life to that of a military soldier.

Through startling shifts in scale and texture, between the snapshot of the youth and the larger "newspaper" image of a soldier in full military fighting gear, the designer has suggested the dramatic changes that the soldier will experience. To further emphasize the departure from his former life, a large swordlike structure moves vertically through the space, cutting the portrait in half. The primary text appears as a banner on this upward-thrusting pole, supported below by a "hand" constructed of text indicating the schedule for the play.

The green line which appears in many of Tartakover's posters represents the pre-1967 border of the state of Israel.

This innovative construction is a prime example of how fragmentation—in this case, the literal cutting of an image by another strong graphic action—can activate a message.

PROJECT
Poster: *Ephraim Returns to the Army*
CLIENT
Neve Tsedek Theatre Group, Yitzchak Laor
Tel Aviv, Israel
DESIGNER
David Tartakover
Tartakover Design
Tel Aviv, Israel

This poster for an exhibit about the social history of life in the Ruhr district of Germany during World War II illustrates the concept of fragmentation in a very direct way. Here the simple act of splitting the title, *Überleben im Krieg* (Surviving at War), makes it appear that it is being broken apart by the image underneath.

The photograph of a concrete bomb shelter with its coarse surface represents the brutality of living through a war experience. The monumentality of the image makes it intimidating and unapproachable, much like the subject of the exhibition. There is no relief from the feeling of oppression when viewing this work. The disruption of the primary text, *Überleben im Krieg*, is a harsh reminder that all who passed through the experience did not really survive intact.

In this poster promoting an exhibition about life in Germany during World War II, the aggression of war is represented by an image that appears to sever the name of the museum exhibit.

PROJECT
Poster: *Überleben im Krieg*
(Surviving at War)
CLIENT
Ruhrlandmuseum Essen
Essen, Germany
DESIGNER
Uwe Loesch
Erkrath, Germany

TEXT FRAGMENTS

"I was frustrated with the self-referential character of my computer, so I went into the garden in order to get an idea." This activated Uwe Loesch's imagination, releasing him from the "trap of repeating earlier solutions." With a new perspective on the problem, he was able to create a very unique announcement for an international exhibition of posters for environmental protection, with the overall title *Grünflächen* (Green Spaces). Loesch's concept for this poster was "typography by coincidence," and the typographic elements, scattered and cut, look like grass clippings, distributed by the natural forces of the wind across the picture plane. The area of dead grass, framed by the lush green of a healthy lawn, indicates the harsh consequences of failing to preserve the environment. This area is proportional to the poster and creates what the designer says is "a poster in a poster for a poster exhibition."

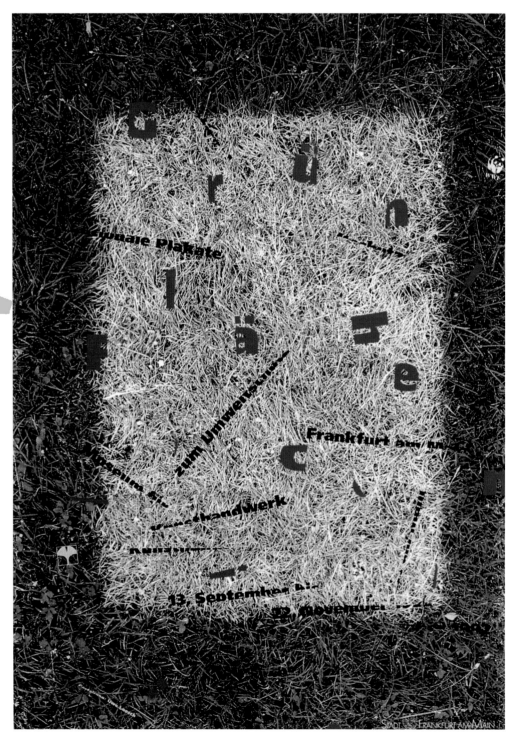

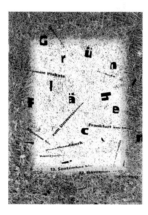

A high-contrast black and white rendering of the poster shows the random fragmentation of the type within the image.

The forces of nature inspired the type/image interaction in this poster about the environment.

PROJECT
Poster: *Grünflächen* (Green Spaces)
CLIENT
Museum für Kunsthandwerk, Frankfurt am Main, Germany
DESIGNER
Uwe Loesch
Erkrath, Germany

A paper shredder provided the means of fragmenting the type for this poster (below left) advertising the German Congress of Historians in Münich, creating a direct force of energy that immediately involves the viewer in the content. This photo-typographic representation of the last-minute destruction of files in 1989 by STASI, the East German secret police, during the unification of East and West Germany perfectly expresses the uncertainties of that historic period.

Uwe Loesch highlighted small pieces of essential information in red type against the spare black and white background. These lines of text are somewhat aligned with the underlying random cut paper, making a bit of order from the chaos.

Using economy of means to achieve its impact, this poster (below right), created for the German political theater group "Das Kom(m)ödchen" demonstrates brilliantly how the cause and effect of text and image can potentially elevate the viewer's level of interest.

The productions in this cabaret-style theater are satires that address controversial subjects—in this case, a performance called *Wokerwanderung* (Migration of Nations) refecting on the tragedy of the Holocaust. Using a simple image of a shower drain from a concentration camp, the designer condensed human suffering into a metaphor. The title, credits, and name of the theater swirl in a pattern that animates the drama of the play: literally "life down the drain."

PROJECT
Poster: *History as an Argument*
CLIENT
41st German Congress of Historians in Munich
Munich, Germany
DESIGNER
Uwe Loesch
Erkrath, Germany

This poster for the German Congress of Historians in Munich achieves an uneasy tension.

PROJECT
Poster: *Migration of Nations*
CLIENT
Political theater group "Das Kom(m)ödchen"
Dusseldorf, Germany
DESIGNER
Uwe Loesch
Erkrath, Germany

This is a vivid example of fragmentation, with strips of type being simply sucked down into the drain in a photograph.

Type becomes suspended
in the power lines in this
common residential alley.

In this photo-typographic
landscape, the bright
yellow type plays with the
image and is affected by
the landscape as it floats
on the water and sets with
the sun.

These posters for Hangul Day in South Korea celebrate the Korean
writing system, Hangul, created in 1446 by King Sejong the Great.
The ingenious system of writing—phonetically accurate and easy to read,
is the official alphabet for the Korean language. Korean typographer and
designer Ahn Sang-Soo, inspired by his fondness for his native language
and its elegant writing system, has devoted himself to the design
problem of adapting Hangul into a series of digital fonts that heighten
its inherent geometrical elegance.

Ahn animated one of his famous typefaces in this poster series celebrating Hangul Day. Giant brightly colored Hangul characters appear to overrun a series of serene black-and-white Korean landscapes. The enormous scale of the letters and their dramatic placement make them appear almost like invaders from outer space, vividly reflecting the designer's sense of humor and imagination. The type/image relationships are exquisitely asymmetric and illustrate the impact of the introduction of Hangul as well as the vitality it has delivered to Korean life.

The type lands from the sky, attaches to buildings along the way, and transports itself down the central road in Seoul.

PROJECT
Posters for Hangul Day
CLIENT
South Korean Ministry of Culture
Seoul, South Korea
DESIGNER
Ahn Sang-Soo
Seoul, Korea

Reza Abedini designed this poster for an exhibition of his students' experimental graphic design work, titled "Type and Image: A Group Exhibition of Type/Image Experiences." The symmetrical layout of the poster, combined with the reverse orientation of the word *Image* at the end of the title, results in a continuous double reading: from left to right as "Type+Image" and from right to left as "Image+Type."

FRAGMENTATION

The "+" sign has been rotated 45 degrees to appear as a multiplication symbol, suggesting the multiple readings that occur when type meets image. The "×" is covering the mouth, implying that design work is "speaking without a mouth."

PROJECT
Poster for exhibition:
"Type and Image"
CLIENT
Azad Art Gallery
Tehran, Iran
DESIGNER
Reza Abedini
Reza Abedini Studio
Tehran, Iran

Reza Abedini is very comfortable working back and forth between type and image. In his cover design for the book *Old Satirical Poetry* (below left), Abedini uses a photograph of a headless Khajeh as the central image to reference the sexual content of the old text without being too explicit.

This group painting exhibition, "Badaneh" (Body), is centered on a particular approach to painting that incorporates primitive calligraphy. The design of the poster (below right) mimics that approach, making calligraphy part of the image. The designer has set poetry in a calligraphic font as well as specific information about the exhibition: the gallery, location, dates, and the names of the artists.

PROJECT
Poster for group
painting exhibition:
"Badaneh" (Body)
CLIENT
Barg Gallery
Tehran, Iran
DESIGNER
Reza Abedini
Reza Abedini Studio
Tehran, Iran

Abedini's posters often incorporate Persian calligraphy and are rendered in earth tones on warm-colored paper, making them rich in both form and meaning.

PROJECT
Book cover:
Old Satirical Poetry
DESIGNER
Reza Abedini
Reza Abedini Studio
Tehran, Iran

The large-scale fountain pen has drawn out the title and come to rest under the arms of the headless figure in the photograph, reinforcing the Khajeh's lack of power.

SIMPLE FRAGMENTATION

The underlying image in this poster, a photograph taken by Man Ray, is inherently fragmented, setting the entire poster by Werner Jeker in motion. Angular, intruding lines are reminiscent of folds in an old photograph, reinforcing the sense of a secret image, chosen by the owner for its special significance. By configuring the type in intervals and angles that mimic the fragmentation in the photograph, the designer has forged a strong connection between the text and image: both interact to define the poster's meaning. The alluring image, while its narrative is ambiguous, invites a wide variety of interpretations.

Hommage   à

du 13 février au 1ᵉʳ avril 1990

Man Ray

Musée de l'Elysée

Lausanne

This project is a prime example of fragmentation used in a highly symbolic way. The image itself has a fractured effect; the designer has simply allowed the text to react to the image's multi-faceted qualities.

PROJECT
Poster: *Hommage à Man Ray*
CLIENT
Musée de l'Elysée Lausanne, Switzerland
DESIGNER
Werner Jeker Les Ateliers du Nord Lausanne, Switzerland
PHOTOGRAPHER
Man Ray

This striking image by the Swiss photographer René Burri, taken at the Ministry of Health in Rio de Janeiro, imposes a powerful awareness of light and motion in an architectural space. The multidirectional light patterns form a dynamic pinwheel effect throughout the image, isolating the human figures and providing areas for the type that make the text an active part of the photographic space. At full scale, this glowing black and white poster might appear as a window into a surreal interactive world of text and image.

This black and white diagram delineates the movement of the light and its directional influence on the placement and reading of the text.

The force of light within this photograph acts as a catalyst for fragmentation.

PROJECT
Poster: *René Burri, Photographies et Collages*
CLIENT
Centre National de la Photographie
Paris, France
DESIGNER
Werner Jeker
Les Ateliers du Nord
Lausanne, Switzerland
PHOTOGRAPHER
René Burri

Simple geometry guides Leonardo Sonnoli's solution for this poster dedicated to the town of Udine. The title, presented in a clean, direct manner, appears in the top half of the composition and is visually cut off from the lower half by two black shapes (portions of the letter *v*, the symbol of Udine). In the lower half, a single photographic image of a statue—shot from a dramatic low angle—sets the interaction among the elements in motion. The statue is one of four that commemorate the branches of the military on the facade of the town's Tempio Ossario di Timau, by the sculptor Silvio Olivo.

The mediating black graphic forms serve two important functions. One reading (the white space) suggests the architectural facade of the memorial that holds the statue. The other reading (the black shapes) is more symbolic, suggesting a cross. Only partially revealed, the sense of a cross is still strong enough to suggest both the statue's location and its relation to the town's history.

This poster is the result of a carefully crafted composition that moves the observer through a monumental white space to define the placement of the type. This is fragmentation at its most subtle.

Arti Grafiche
Friulane 80°
Dedicato a Udine
CODEsign

Tempio-Ossario (1925-40)
arch. P. Valle-A. Limongelli
statue di S. Olivo (1938-50)

The statue initiates the discourse among the elements, but the white space is the dominant force that fragments the message.

PROJECT
Poster: Dedicato a Udine
(Dedicated to Udine)
CLIENT
Town of Udine, Italy
DESIGNER
**Leonardo Sonnoli
CODEsign
Rimini, Italy**

Fragmented graphic and
typographic elements find
their motivating source in
the central photograph by
Paul Strand.

PROJECT
Poster: La Luce Incisa
(The Light Engraved)
CLIENT
City of Chiasso
Chiasso, Switzerland
DESIGNER
Bruno Monguzzi
Meride, Switzerland
PHTOGRAPHER
Paul Strand

For a photographic exhibition, designer Bruno Monguzzi carefully
considered photography's principal issues: light and the translation of
light into indexical symbols. Monguzzi located a photograph by the
American photographer Paul Strand in the middle of the poster and then
imagined the type responding to the photo's dynamic composition.

The energy created by the placement of the photograph has literally
pushed the large graphic forms, slashes of white space, and layered
typography into the upper portion of the composition. Each element
appears to be reacting individually as well as initiating separate responses
from every portion of the composition. The observer cannot help but
become totally involved in the poster's energy.

The relationship between type and image sets up a captivating tension between systematic and organic relationships.

Yuri Gulitov's love of the Cyrillic alphabet and its highly original forms inspire his typeface designs as well as his method of combining type with image. Often the letterforms mirror the shapes of objects. In this poster designed for an exhibition of his fonts, for example, the largest letter on the poster resembles a loudspeaker or floodlight that's broadcasting the type from the lower left corner. (The letter looks like *KD* but sounds like "yu" in English.) The energy of unrestrained street creativity—graffiti, inscriptions on fences, handmade announcements, and market signs are other influences that come to the surface in Gulitov's lively posters.

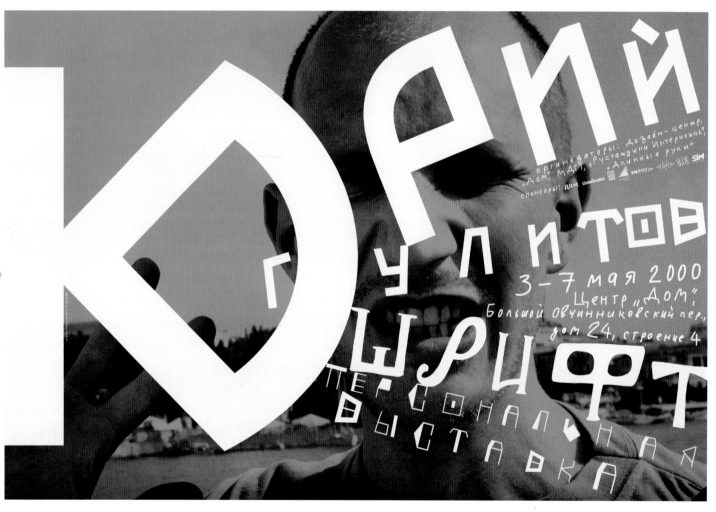

PROJECT
Poster for exhibition of Yuri Gulitov's typefaces
CLIENT
Self
DESIGNER
Yuri Gulitov
Moscow, Russia
PHOTOGRAPHER
Ekaterina Gulitova

This poster for a one-man show of typefaces makes a strong connection between the designer and his unpredictable alphabets.

The diagrammatic rendering of the poster (opposite) shows how the large word *Yuri* intersects with the portrait of Yuri. The first letter interlocks with his ear, the second aligns with his nose and head; and the last two are angled with his eye to make a connection between his face and the typeface. This sets up an initial expectation of order that gradually gives way to fragmentation as the smaller type becomes progressively more disconnected from the image. The energy of the handwritten letters breaking away and moving in front of the designer reinforces the fluidity between Yuri and his creative process.

PROJECT
Poster for exhibition: "Design '99"
CLIENT
Designers Union of Russia
DESIGNER/
PHOTOGRAPHER
**Yuri Gulitov
Moscow, Russia**

This poster for the all-Russian competition Design '99, shows how the atmosphere in a photo can appear to affect the placement of type.

A similar poster (above) for a Russian Design Competition exhibition also uses a letterform as a starting point. Here the designer plays off the resemblance of the Russian letter *D* to a chair, a designed object appropriate to the subject. The "chair" appears multiple times against the sky. Again there is a feeling of spontaneity and discontinuity as the white letterforms splinter away from the image to create fragmented counterforms. With both of these posters, Gulitov composed the type first and then married it with a pre-existing image.

PROJECT
Poster for clothing
retailer Ba-Tsu
CLIENT
Ba-Tsu Co., Ltd.
Tokyo, Japan
DESIGNER
Makoto Saito
Makoto Saito Design
Office, Inc.
Tokyo, Japan

This poster by Makoto
Saito implies that
shopping at the Japanese
retailer Ba-Tsu will be
lively and full of the
unexpected.

The use of implied motion to emphasize a point can be an extremely
effective tool in the hands of an experienced and creative designer such
as Makoto Saito. This poster (above), designed for the Japanese apparel
retailer Ba-Tsu, is a very whimsical representation of the shopping
experience. Repeated letterforms spelling out the store's name appear to
be "flying" through the picture plane.

A large face (perhaps of a shopper) peers in through the implied three-
dimensional space from outside, adding a further sense of mystery and
surprise to the composition. Animated gestures, color, and a balanced
asymmetrical composition combine to form a powerful and sophisticated
solution. By fragmenting the informational text and distorting the
viewer's sense of scale, Saito has successfully implied that shopping in
this particular store is a dynamic personal experience.

For the American Institute of Graphic Arts (AIGA) in San Francisco, Jean-Benoît Lévy created this poster for The Seam, a tour of nine design studios in the Bay Area. (In mining terminology, a seam is a stratum of mineral deposits.)

The single photograph of a model wearing theatrical paint adds a sense of mystery and drama. The colored diamonds, which represent each studio, appear to float suspended above the surface of the black and white photo. By emphasizing these forms, the designer has created a feeling that the model is in fact looking into each gem, seeing what participants in the tour will discover—nine diverse and highly inventive studios. The AIGA wrote of this tour: "Welcome to The Seam. This is the place where heat, pressure, and processing speed combine to form delicate gems of creativity."

By choosing to scatter the diamonds, number them, and reproduce them in a range of color variations, the designer has constructed a specialized code system within the context of the poster. The exact meaning isn't apparent to the viewer on first encounter; it requires some decoding and contemplation, making it ultimately a very rewarding experience.

PROJECT
Poster: *The Seam*
CLIENT
AIGA
San Francisco, USA
DESIGNER
Jean-Benoît Lévy
Studio AND (Trafic Grafic)
Basel, Switzerland/
San Francisco, USA
PHOTOGRAPHER
Robert Schlatter
San Francisco, USA
MODEL
Jen Huggans @ Look
Model Agency
San Francisco, USA

In this mysterious composition, the type floats on colored gems, representing nine San Francisco design studios that will be part of the tour the poster is promoting.

Type and image reconfigure to form two distinct compositions celebrating the life and work of the distinguished Japanese designer Yusaku Kamekura.

PROJECT
Poster: *Sunrise Sunset*
Yusaku Kamekura
CLIENT
Toppan Printing Co. Ltd.
Tokyo, Japan
DESIGNER
Makoto Saito
Makoto Saito Design
Office, Inc.
Tokyo, Japan

To honor the passing of his good friend and fellow graphic designer Yusaku Kamekura, Makoto Saito created these two assemblages. "He played the role of the sun," the designer states, referencing Kamekura's landmark sun flag design for the 1964 Olympic games in Japan. Saito skillfully integrated a portrait, the red circle of the "sun," and numerous framing devices to illustrate the beginning and end of a life in graphic design.

The multiple black lines surrounding the portrait add to the impression of Kamekura's presence as a creative influence, viewing the world in terms of the frame of the printed page. By fragmenting these structures, Makoto Saito has activated the picture plane and has successfully represented Kamekura's life force.

Both the sunrise and sunset pieces appear to be based to a degree on ritual, that is, the careful arrangement of objects and images in relation to each other. Each element and its location within the context of the poster references cultural traditions—for example, the placement of the "sun" in either the top third or bottom third of each composition represents life (top third) and death (bottom third).

Kamekura's expression in his portrait, the symbols of the sun, and the multiplicity suggested in the frame construction combine to form a strong personal narrative. The duality of the two compositions is a positive reflection on a life lived and a life that will continue to live through his work.

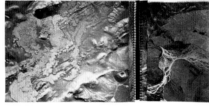

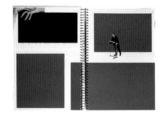

Through the use of collage, spiral binding, fold outs, and expressive interaction of type and image, the designers have extended the experience of the Olafur Eliasson pavilion.

This book, designed by cyan, is intended as an extension rather than simply a representation of the project on which it is based. That work was the Blind Pavilion, conceived and built by the much-acclaimed Danish artist Olafur Eliasson.

Constructed for the fiftieth Venice biennial, one of the most important contemporary art exhibitions in Europe, the pavilion that Eliasson created was a mixed-media installation comprising "mirror reflections, glass kaleidoscopes, light works, running staircases, architectonic interventions, and camera obscura." As an integral part of the total experience, he also wanted a book that would be "a visually and textually fascinating labyrinth, far beyond a traditional exhibition catalogue."

Eliasson chose cyan for the design, and their challenge was to extend the visual experience of the pavilion, as well as to invent a book/construct for the collection of writings authored by Danish writer Svend Age Madsen and ten international writers and theoreticians. The resulting design, with spiral binding and four different types of paper, is a "loop" that has no discernible beginning or end and perfectly showcases the multifaceted journey of the text, making a captivating continuum for the reader.

Cyan used a number of design devices on these complex pages (opposite), including interlocking and overlapping elements, color overlays, moving text elements, and a wide variety of images. Some represent the actual architectural structure of the pavilion, and others are more suggestive of the content—but all converge to express the essential ideas.

An invisible magnetic force seems to have an effect on the text elements throughout. For example in the spread below, the left page contains what at first appears to be a series of paragraphs in disarray. Upon closer examination, viewers are treated to a short narrative (curiously written in the first person) concerning the possible origins of language, about a tribe's "discovery" of their first word. The form of the fragmented text is clearly expressing the upheaval felt by the tribe as they recognized the power of words.

The right page on the same spread contains an overhead view of a person whose hands and arms appear to be in motion, and possibly operating a small handheld device. A yellow triangular field converges toward the person from the text on the left page, implying either that he is trying to control the unruly paragraphs or that they are directly affecting him. This yellow field appears throughout the publication, both to serve as a formal unifying element and to reflect the level of interactivity, or cause and effect, between the images and the text.

PROJECT
Book: *Olafur Eliasson,*
The Blind Pavilion
CLIENT
Danish Contemporary
Art Foundation
Copenhagen, Denmark
DESIGNERS
Detlef Fiedler and
Daniela Haufe
cyan
Berlin, Germany

The text on the left page describes the formation of language. The small seated figure on the right page appears to be setting the text in motion. The yellow "force field," a design element that appears throughout the book, interferes with conventional type placement.

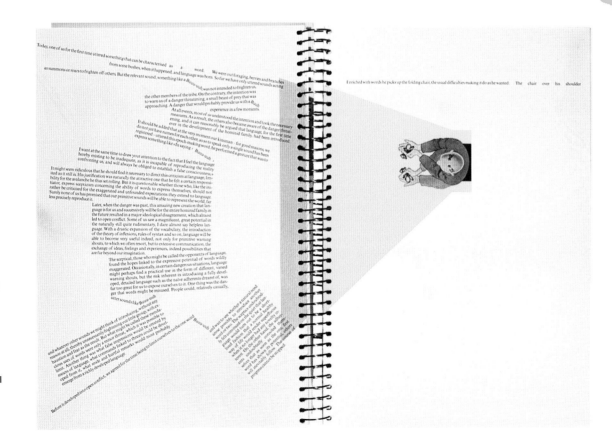

This spread delivers its message by representing a lecture space. The image of a man behind a folding podium faces the text on the opposite page, which reads, "When with one hand he steers the folding chair past other guest, other beholders, and with the other feels to make sure the booklet is still in its place."

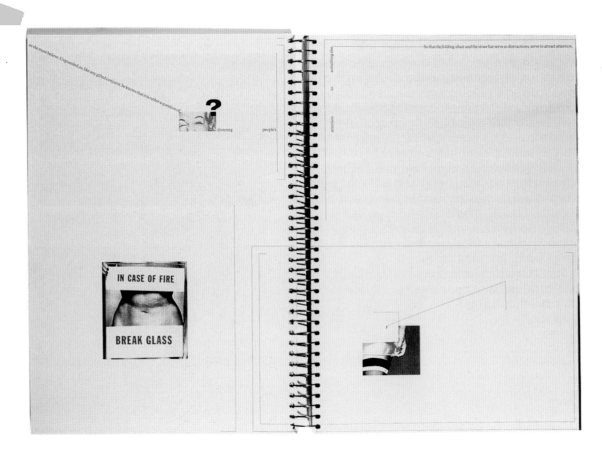

IN CASE OF FIRE

BREAK GLASS

A page of exquisitely composed white space contains minimal text: "Unguarded, as, like any gifted conjuror, he knows that it is rather a question of directing people's attention to something else."

These spreads graphically translate the structure of one part of the pavilion where multifaceted triangles allow visitors to see themselves (or parts of themselves) as though peering into a kaleidoscope.

COLOR PAPER
WARM

Cut-up scrap paper
was used to generate
compositions.

The designers began
building collage
compositions (below
right) by folding pieces
of architectural plans,
letterforms, text, and
landscape around images
of a human figure—
exploring the relationship
between architecture, the
body, and typography.

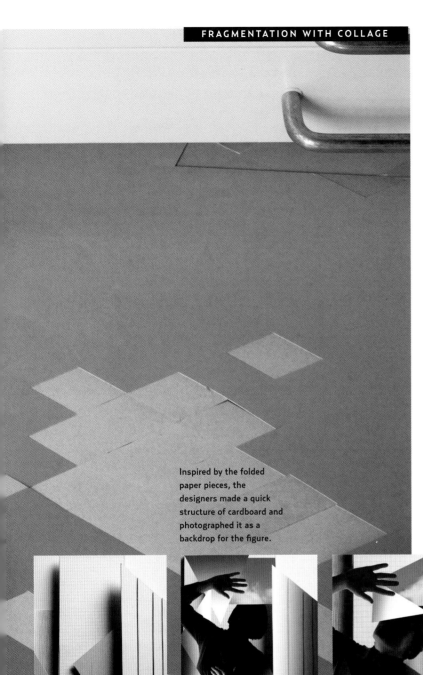

The relationships among type, image, and message must be continuously integrated from the beginning of the design process. Collage is often a fertile starting point that leads immediately to experimental relationships between pictures and text.

The 2005 Lyceum Competition theme, "Smart Materials, Wearable Architecture," provided endless visual inspiration for structures, textures, and gestures. Because the creative process is intuitive and needs to flow quickly from initial thought to execution, it is important to begin making form without any preconceptions first, and then later step back and evaluate. To ensure there would be plenty of material to work with, the designers shot many poses of a figure in front of a digital camera and then began juxtaposing the human form with the collage material. They worked back and forth between figure and background to create a seamless photomontage, which flowed from the body to the structure to the typography.

As the body and the structure became one, bits of type from the original collages began to suggest possible type placements. Each year's poster must feature the date as a dominant element. Also, numerals are easy to read, and operate on a slightly different level of communication than letters and words, so they are easier to abstract. The designers took a cue from the large letterforms folding around the edges of the geometric shape at the top of one of the earlier collages.

Inspired by the folded paper pieces, the designers made a quick structure of cardboard and photographed it as a backdrop for the figure.

Several compositions were made very quickly. The more the figure became wrapped with the structure, the more it connoted the theme of wearable architecture.

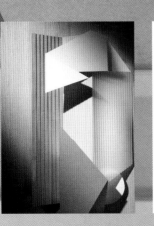

The final photographic composition (left) shows how the photomontage flowed seamlessly from the body to the structure.

The final background model (far left) was crafted from woodgrain paper, balsa wood, and corrugated plastic and mounted on FomeCor®.

C

traveling

5

c

fellowship

2

...ctural Center

Chicago

wearable

J u r y:

Jennifer Siegal, Principal
Author and Chair
Office of Mobile design
Venice, California
Professor, Woodbury College

Alanna Stang
Executive Editor, ID Magazine
New York, New York

Andrew Blauvelt
Design Director, Walker Art Center
Minneapolis, Minnesota

Amy Christie Anderson, Principal
ACAlects
Honolulu, Hawaii

Many of the unexpected fragments of text in the final poster were the direct result of lucky accidents that occurred during the collage process. This collage (right top) sparked the structure for the folding pieces of type and sky around the head.

For the final type configuration, the designers traced the folded form at the top of the image and inverted it to make a framework for the primary text. A sequence of windows in perspective, left over from earlier experiments, also found a place in the final typographic grid. These provided baselines and defined areas for the letterforms of the word *Lyceum* and the program title. The designers created a connecting line between the top and bottom grid structures to locate secondary text.

Tracing and flipping the geometric forms in the photograph gave the designers the basis for the typographic grid for small pieces of text.

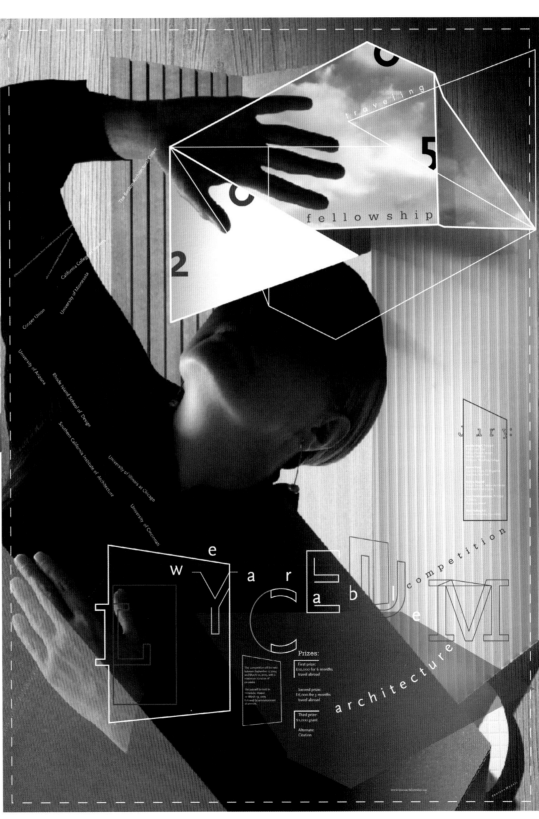

PROJECT
Poster for annual student architecture competition
CLIENT
Lyceum Fellowship
Cambridge, Massachusetts, USA
DESIGNERS
Nancy Skolos and Thomas Wedell
Skolos-Wedell
Canton, Massachusetts, USA
PHOTOGRAPHER
Thomas Wedell
Canton, Massachusetts, USA

For the "Lichtecht" exhibition at the Museum für Gestaltung in Zurich, centered on light and its effects on everyday objects, Martin Woodtli assembled an elaborate construction of reflective letterforms, lighting, and signage. Each object acts independently while simultaneously functioning within the entire picture plane to form a unified message. The strong contrast from dark to light in the photographic assemblage, and the intense colored light, conveys the theme of the show, and electronic signage simultaneously relay the specifics of the time, place, and dates.

The constructed type elements convey information and also represent what viewers might encounter in the exhibition—familiar objects that reflect, project, emit, or fragment light.

PROJECT
Poster for exhibition:
Lichtecht
CLIENT
Museum für Gestaltung
Zurich, Switzerland
DESIGNER
Martin Woodtli
Zurich, Switzerland

To announce the presentation of "VideoEx," an international experimental film and video competition held each year in Zurich, Woodtli created a matrix of video scan lines as the backdrop for the typographic elements in the poster. By distorting and degrading the legibility with the raster bands, he makes the viewer aware of both the experimental nature of the presentations and the almost tactile quality of the medium itself.

This digital energy impacts every element in the poster, including the type. Technical drawings of artifacts from various kinds of media—film, video, and sound recording—in combination with dimensional markings reinforce the engineered quality of this piece.

Video scanning fragments both image and text in this hyper-animated poster for a video competition.

PROJECT
Poster: *VideoEx*
CLIENT
**Kunstraum Walcheturm
Zurich, Switzerland**
DESIGNER
**Martin Woodtli
Zurich, Switzerland**

FRAGMENTATION

A system of reflection, constants, and variables sets up a dialogue between the objective and subjective aspects of music.

Art Direction: Allen Hori
Photography: Doubt's Shadow: Gaye Chan, Professor of Photography, University of Hawaii at Manoa
Photography: cover and color images: Allen Hori
Words and Language: Augustine Hope
Design: Allen Hori
Series planning and coordination: The Kuester Group, Minneapolis, Minnesota
Design: Sidebar Treat: Charlie Becker, Executive Senior Designer Concerning Matters of Advertising, Atlantic Records, New York
Design: Sticky Rubber Typography: Rob Eberhardt, Cyber Wizard, Atlantic Records, New York

Vintage Remarque. 50% Total Recovered Fiber 10% Post-Consumer Fiber

Potlatch Potlatch Corporation
Northwest Paper Division
Cloquet, Minnesota 55720
©1994 Potlatch Corporation

PROJECT
Poster promoting Potlatch
Vintage Remarque
Paper
CLIENT
Potlatch Corporation
Spokane, Washington,
USA
DESIGNER
Allen Hori
Bates Hori
New York, USA
PHOTOGRAPHERS
Allen Hori and Gaye Chan
New York, USA

Multiple, superimposed images of a ladder may be interpreted as series of ascending scales. The repetition affects the relationship of the type's placement to the image. The bottom portion contains even more complex encoding.

Allen Hori chose music as the theme for a series of pieces to introduce a new line of paper for Potlatch Corporation. The immediately apparent unifying element is the evenly divided composition. The designer set up this format in order to "express the duality of music, the internal and external aspects of sound." The structure provides a backdrop for many complex type/image relationships. Each panel contains one word as part of the system that initiates the viewer's interpretation of each piece. These words—*repose, reverie,* and *rescind*—are skillfully placed to augment the meaning of the many fragmented elements.

In the first panel, "Repose" (opposite), the upper half is occupied by the rendition of a house constructed from a carpenter's ruler. This reference to a built structure is a metaphor for the mathematical composition of music. The text that lists the credits for the paper promotion is placed at intervals that are somewhat aligned with the folding ruler. In the lower half of the piece, an assemblage of objects forms a nebulous mass that contrasts with the calculated nature of the top half and illustrates the unpredictable forces at work in the creative act of music making. The text leads the viewer into the mythological origins of music, and further into music's subjective and introspective nature. ("Echo fell in love with Narcissus. When her love was not returned, she pined away until only her voice remained.") It also reveals a possible source of inspiration for the mirrored format and echoing of messages in the series.

The other two panels (right) also have dual natures. The creation of a dialogue between their upper and lower halves allowed the designer to express both the informational and psychological points of view as well as to set up an enigmatic tension between them. He has included more than enough images and symbols to ponder and to associate, taking this series into a very advanced aesthetic realm.

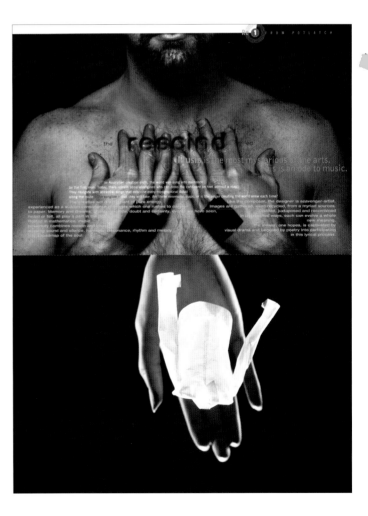

This panel, "Rescind," deals with the inner and outer worlds of the musician. In the top half, a man's hands are held close to his heart. In the bottom half, a glowing white shirt is a symbol of the conformity that is sometimes necessary to succeed.

For the Eighth Annual Edition of *The Alternative Pick*, a directory of creative professionals, Allen Hori developed a graphic language that requires a great deal of decoding in order to identify and appreciate all the embedded information. Here fragmentation operates on both a visual and symbolic level. Signs are intermixed and can be decoded individually or assembled to construct additional meanings. It is as if Hori has developed his own grammar from which he assembles a metalanguage of words, pictures, and symbols.

Designed to be displayed in multiples and linked horizontally to form a sequence of infinity symbols, the poster sets up the viewer's initial encounter with Hori's cryptic language. Looking at a single poster, the symbol is incomplete and resembles a piece of fruit or a droplet of liquid. The bottom half of the drop appears to be contained in an eggshell, and a blue-green pattern emerging from the background evokes a scientific aura that projects a life force from its center onto the egg, as if to underscore its creation.

ETH8R 5

www.altpick.com
The Alternative Pick 8th Annual Edition
© 1999 STORM MUSIC ENTERTAINMENT, INC.

BATES HORI, NEW YORK

The visual system of linking the posters to form the infinity symbol reinforces the mission of the directory, which is to connect creative people.

PROJECT
Poster and catalog:
The Alternative Pick
CLIENT
**Storm Music
Entertainment
New York, USA**
DESIGNER
**Allen Hori
Bates Hori
New York, USA**

Inside the catalog, the level of discovery and the increased complexity of images and text continue to invite the reader to systematically construct meaning based on the "evidence" held within the pages.

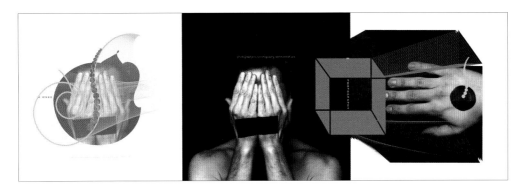

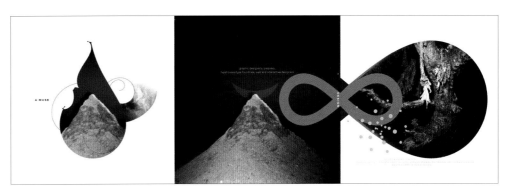

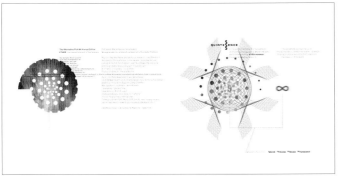

The pages of the catalog contain sporadic lines of isolated, subjective thoughts centered on the human spirit, such as "looking for movement in shadow—the truth may lie in half-light." These brief but thought-provoking insertions spark the reader's imagination and encourage creative activity.

The designer adds continuity to the structure of the piece through the repeated use of creative, generative symbology such as the egg, flower, and infinity symbol.

The mythical nature of Ed Fella's drawings and typographic exercises is a continuous source of material for design theorists to draw upon and interpret. Despite his predisposition for the world of the vernacular, his imagination still manages to bridge the two worlds of "high" and "low" culture, leading to complex designs with many interpretations. His experimentation with type and image is remarkably fluid, and there is always an animated dialogue between the two.

For a presentation of his work in Rotterdam, Fella prepared one of his "after-the-fact" fliers. He distributes these pieces only at lectures or as follow-up reminders of events. This one is a blueprint of Fella's stream of consciousness as he interpreted Dutch culture. From his prankish hand-drawn version of a font originally created by Theo van Doesburg to farcical renderings of a windmill, wooden shoe, and a tulip, the piece provides multiple points of entry into Dutch culture as well as a window into Fella's exceptional imagination.

PROJECT
Poster for Dutch lecture
CLIENT
Self
DESIGNER
Ed Fella
Valencia, California, USA

Ed Fella's panorama of type and images is part poster, part landscape, and part de Stijl.

This post-event memento for National Design Awards finalists (including Fella) has a surreal quality. Fella translated an image of an American landscape and added hand-drawn text that appears to be growing out of the image. By rendering both the text and the image in similar line weights, Fella establishes an immediate visual connection between the American designers and their homeland. However, by placing their names to the right and above the image in progressively more remote positions, he seems to be making a statement that the design award finalists have established a unique position at the edges of the profession.

This small flier is an example of Fella's introspective approach to design. The arrangement of unrelated elements, some photographic, some hand drawn, offer the viewer few clues as to Fella's exact meaning. Again, close observation furnishes some clues, but the final explanation in Fella's own words is that it represents "the idea of my archive of stuff with all its bits and pieces that I have to see to someday."

PROJECT
Flier for National Design Awards
CLIENT
Self
DESIGNER
Ed Fella
Valencia, California, USA

Names of the three finalists for the Cooper-Hewitt National Design Award frame the top right corner of a drawing, positioning them outside the boundaries of the design profession.

PROJECT
Things I Gotta Do Today flier
CLIENT
Self
DESIGNER
Ed Fella
Valencia, California, USA

A large human eye initiates multiple points of entry into a complex arrangement of type and image for the viewer to ponder.

Martin Woodtli created this flier to promote upcoming events at Kunstkanal, an alternative gallery in Bern, Switzerland. Because of the unconventional nature of the gallery's exhibitions, the designer has taken the opportunity to experiment, and he exploits this freedom completely.

Woodtli establishes the feeling of movement across the width of the piece by flipping and mirroring elements, beginning the messages in opposing corners. Further motion is activated on a layer containing supporting information with linear graphics in a lighter color behind. The combination of the two layers creates a lateral gesture resembling an electronic message board. This illusory force acts on each element to create a range of size variations and random distortions in a state of endless flux.

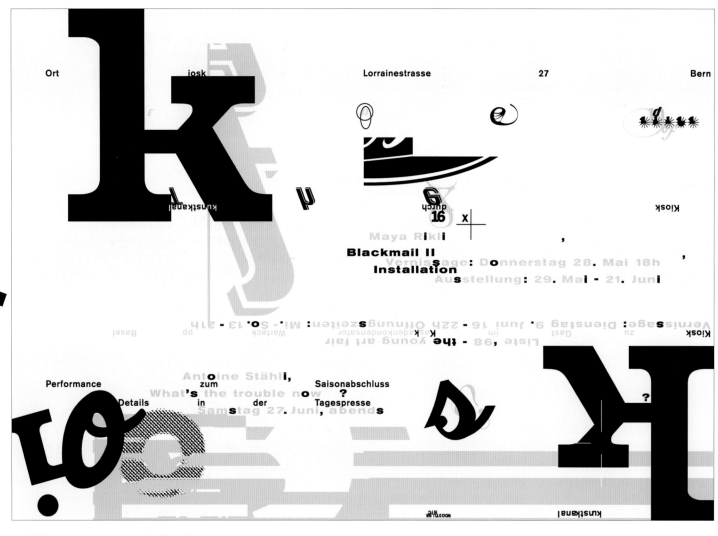

PROJECT
Flier for kiosk: *Blackmail*
CLIENT
Kunstkanal
Bern, Switzerland
DESIGNER
Martin Woodtli
Zurich, Switzerland

Martin Woodtli applies fragmented type and form to animate a flier announcing upcoming events at an alternative art gallery.

The Swedish magazine, *Soda*, publishes articles about visual culture written by a variety of authors. Taking this as a starting point, the designer created this cover design using a combination of techniques. Hand-drawn letterforms mix seamlessly with type constructed of automotive muffler parts while anatomical drawings of horses wallpaper the background. In addition, an organic "river" winds its way through the middle of the composition, terminating in the lower portion of the layout as it loosely reconfigures into animal faces.

The designer is less concerned with clarity of meaning than with energizing the reader's imagination, and inviting the reader to look inside the magazine to discover the multifarious nature of the content.

This lighthearted combination of miscellany sets the stage for a publication with many divergent points of view.

PROJECT
Soda Magazine cover:
Multi
CLIENT
Soda Magazine
DESIGNER
**Martin Woodtli
Zurich, Switzerland**

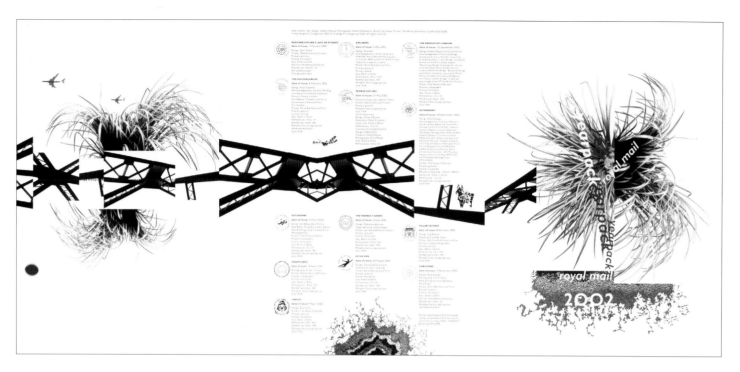

"Design in connection with postage stamps and coinage may be described, I think, as the silent ambassadors on national taste," wrote the poet W. B. Yeats. This quote is a starting point in Siobhan Keaney's design of this annual folder that features all the special-edition stamps issued by the Royal Mail, to establish the importance of a thoughtful design strategy for all government communications.

This piece is certainly no exception. To commemorate the year's collection, Keaney has created a fragmented collage of images that spans the layout completely, depicting only small suggestive portions of the subjects on the various stamps. By placing the stamp descriptions in either a parallel or perpendicular relationship to the active image space, Keaney has maintained the clarity and detail required for the text.

PROJECT
Royal Mail year pack folder
CLIENT
Royal Mail
London, UK
DESIGNER
Siobhan Keaney
London, UK

Fragmented images of bridges, one of the themes in the Royal Mail special-edition stamps, provide the underpinning for this montage. Some of the other subjects commemorated in this folder for the Royal Mail are "Coastline," "Peter Pan," "Circus," "Christmas," "Airliners," and "Astronomy."

PROJECT
Poster/flier for Millkybar
CLIENT
The Mill
London, UK
DESIGNER
Siobhan Keaney
London, UK

Colorful images collide with strong typography to fragment the picture plane of this poster, implying that the Millkybar is a highly energetic place.

Activity is at the heart of this poster/flier for the Millkybar, an in-house café at the Mill, a state-of-the-art video editing company in London. The fragmented arrangement of the text and its accompanying graphic elements further the sensation of animation. The designer has interspersed hand-drawn representations of a milk glass and coffee cup with photographic images of a cow and kitchen utensils, creating a sense of place. The use of the color red to accent selected graphic elements both heightens the level of activity already present and highlights some of the essential information.

A multifaceted street
scene sets up a discourse
between imagination and
reality in this poster for a
children's theater festival.

PROJECT
Poster: *La tête dans les
nuages festival de
spectacles pour les
enfants et leurs parents*
(The Head in the Clouds
Festival for Children and
Their Parents)
CLIENT
Théâtre d'Angoulême
Angoulême, France
DESIGNER
Anette Lenz
Vincent Perrottet
Paris, France

To promote the annual La Tête dans les Nuages (Head in the Clouds) festival in Angoulême, France, Anette Lenz has created a highly imaginative and whimsical series of promotional materials. The first (opposite) juxtaposes two images in a curious, split scenario: the top is a pastoral landscape and the bottom is a crowded urban street scene. Cascading white "confetti," which interacts with the animated typography, sets a celebratory tone. The size variations in the type create the illusion of depth—as if the words are being broadcasted from the treetops to publicize the upcoming festival to the urban dwellers below.

A human figure diving into a night sky, represents the idea that attending a new season at the theater is like plunging into the unknown. As a backdrop, the designer constructed multilayered landscapes—stacked, asymmetrically sandwiched assemblies that fluctuate throughout the series (below). The background image, a summer landscape, establishes a deep sense of space behind the middle ground, which comprises black and white graphic and typographic elements. In another piece from the series (below left), the designer extended the process of layering by cropping the original poster image and introducing a new background photograph. This forces the perspective even further, fabricating a dreamscape that heightens the audience's expectations for the season.

The blackness of space in the center of the composition is surrounded by sunlit landscape, making this poster into a metaphor for the dramatic range of stage productions (right).

An additional background layer takes the audience farther into an implied window of endless variation (above).

PROJECT
Poster and invitation for the 2002–03 season
CLIENT
Théâtre d'Angoulême Angoulême, France
DESIGNER
Anette Lenz
Vincent Perrottet
Paris, France

FRAGMENTATION

In this poster for an architecture competition, fragmentation is used to represent the program for designing an urban residential penthouse.

PROJECT
Poster for annual student architecture competition
CLIENT
Lyceum Fellowship
Cambridge,
Massachusetts, USA
DESIGNERS
Thomas Wedell and
Nancy Skolos
Skolos-Wedell
Canton, Massachusetts,
USA
PHOTOGRAPHER
Thomas Wedell
Canton, Massachusetts,
USA

The Lyceum Fellowship poster for 2006 required a multilevel approach in order to represent an intricate architectural program, calling for the design of a prefabricated, energy-efficient urban penthouse for a family of four, atop a multistory building in the historic financial district of Boston, Massachusetts.

Several motivational forces are in operation throughout the poster. First and foremost is a structural reference to the program's theme, expressed in the construction of an abstract (reductive) model that mimics a bird's eye view of Boston's densely packed financial district. The model is an exaggeration—relying on steep angles, condensed spaces, and forced perspective—to achieve the sensation of flying over the urban space. The structure in the lower half of the picture plane represents a rooftop, the designated construction site. Through the use of pattern and texture, the designers have given a transitional look to this portion of the composition, alluding to the proposed changes yet to come. Embedded in this primary image are additional photographs, intended as representations of the urban architectural environment to strengthen the concepts expressed in the program and add more dynamic architecture to the poster.

The designers placed diagrammatical graphic elements that reference the photographic structure on a layer above, and flipped them horizontally to extend the rooftop space. This linear framework is presented in both white and yellow; the yellow shapes match the shape of the penthouse site and appear to be plan drawings. This provides the force that informs the placement of the text. Essential words locate themselves both within their own syntax and in relation to the total composition, creating an overall effect of fragmentation.

In contrast, the placement of the Lyceum logo demonstrates how more than one kind of text/image relationship can be created within a single piece. In this part of the poster, the black background image and the three-dimensional letters have been photographed to achieve a fusion of the logo and the structure. This anchoring of the logo was intentional, because it represents the sponsor of the fellowship; other elements relating to the specific program change each year.

Diagrammatical graphic elements that reference the photographic image further activate the space and mediate the type.

Collage sketches (left) explored various spatial relationships and points of view.

The pressure of a jury review is implied by placing the jurors' names near a wooden press.

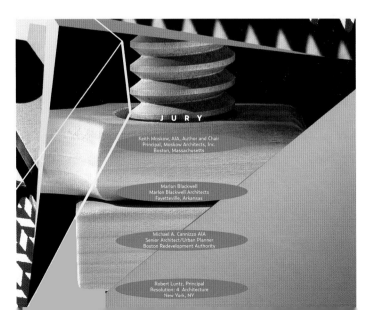

JURY

Keith Moskow, AIA, Author and Chair
Principal, Moskow Architects, Inc.
Boston, Massachusetts

Marlon Blackwell
Marlon Blackwell Architects
Fayetteville, Arkansas

Michael A. Cannizzo AIA
Senior Architect/Urban Planner
Boston Redevelopment Authority

Robert Luntz, Principal
Resolution: 4 Architecture
New York, NY

LYCEUM

Three-dimensional letters were fabricated from plastic, then painted and photographed in perspective.

The designers edited the collages and chose this as the final composition, which most resembled a roof (below).

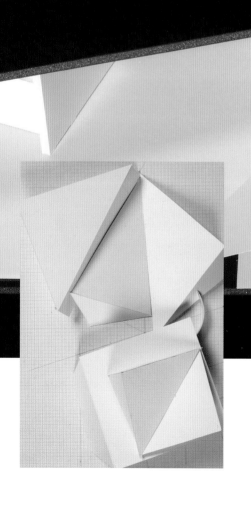

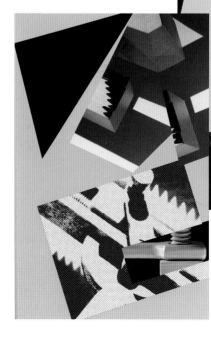

A rough paper model (right) was constructed based on the final collage sketch (left).

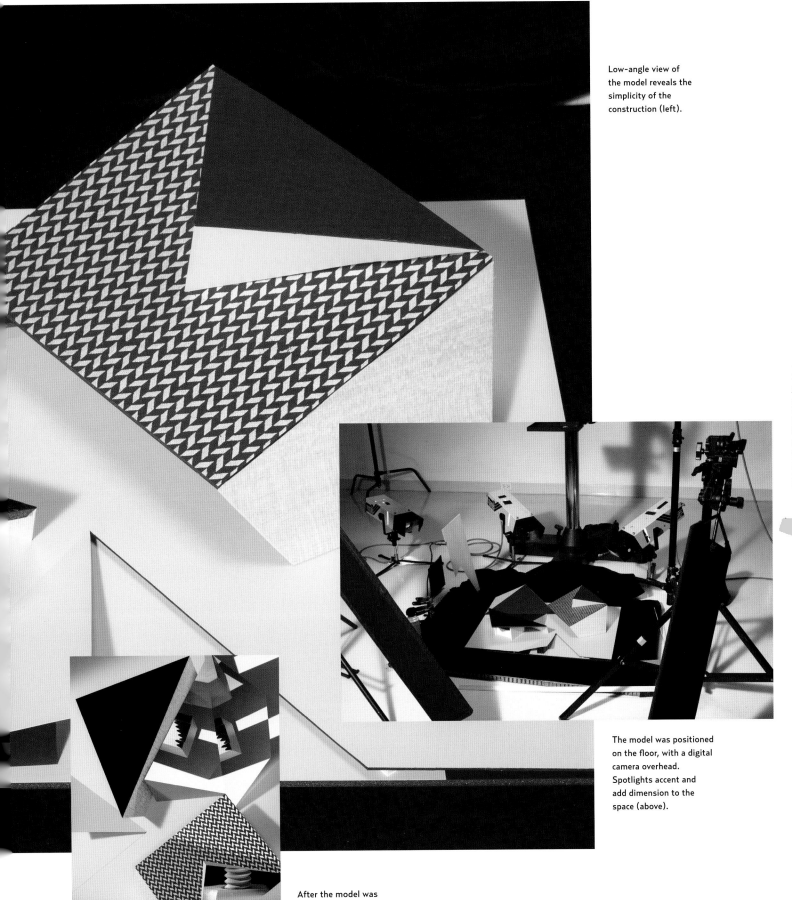

Low-angle view of
the model reveals the
simplicity of the
construction (left).

The model was positioned
on the floor, with a digital
camera overhead.
Spotlights accent and
add dimension to the
space (above).

After the model was
photographed, additional
images were combined in
Adobe Photoshop (left).

INVERSION

Type and image trade roles

Inversion is a specific category of fusion, in which type and image fuse by exchanging roles. As with fusion, the relationship that takes place in inversion is similar to a chemical reaction with two substances bonding together. When type is portrayed as part of an image, or when an image is built from type, it captures our imagination and transports us beyond the potential communicative properties of type or image alone and into an elevated sense of discovery.

Applications

To reveal a potential or un-
realized connection among
elements and ideas

To create harmony and
integration among different or
related texts by blending them
into a visual union

To generate visual or verbal
puns, or both

To invent fictional narratives
between words and images,
where words and letterforms
become the characters

To create the strongest
possible connection between
the word and the image

Formal qualities

Hyper-realism

The type is physically
photographed or rendered
through other hyper-realistic
means.

Building blocks

The letterforms appear within
the picture plane as the building
blocks from which the image is
constructed.

Frames

The letters create frames for
preexisting photographic
images.

Image as Type

PROJECT
Poster series
CLIENT
**Università Iuav di
Venezia, Architecture
Venice, Italy**
DESIGNER
**Leonardo Sonnoli
CODEsign
Rimini, Italy**

**This sequence of sketches
shows Sonnoli's develop-
ment of the type/image
relationship.**

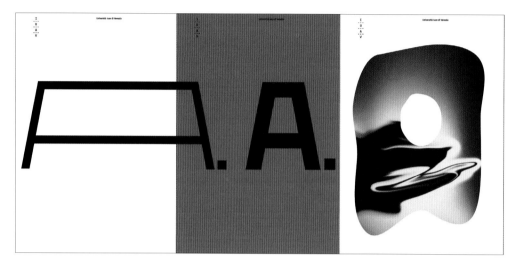

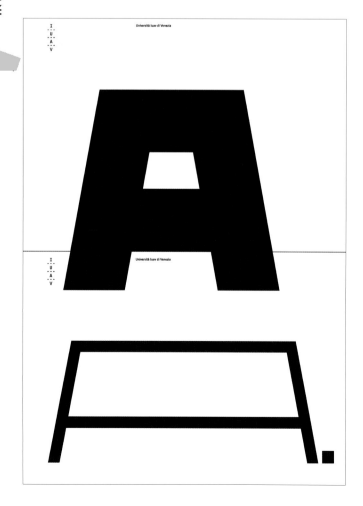

Leonardo Sonnoli is one of the masters of conveying a message economically. His posters use dramatic white space where letterforms are often the key players.

Sonnoli created this poster (below) to mark the beginning of the academic year (*anno accademico*) at the Università Iuav in Venice. He constructed the monumental composition from only four ingredients: a capital letter *A*, a square period, a triangle implying another *A*, and a close-up photograph of water. The substitution of the water photograph for the outline

of the letter *A* not only places the school on a canal in Venice but also creates an energetic interaction and state of flux among the architectural and typographic elements in the poster. The water is shaped by a large letterform *A* that is so immense it bleeds off the page. Even though the designer didn't intentionally plan it, the white counterform inside the water suggests the shape of the front of a gondola. This flickering back and forth between the typographic and photographic invites viewer participation and lends delight and discovery to the experience of reading the message.

With only a few skillfully arranged elements and many subtle interrelationships among them, this poster sets the stage for celebration, reflection, and interaction.

PROJECT
Posters for 32º Huesca Film Festival in Huesca, Spain
CLIENT
Huesca Film Festival
DESIGNER
Leonardo Sonnoli
CODEsign
Rimini, Italy

These dramatic posters for the Huesca Film festival are staged and lit much like a film production.

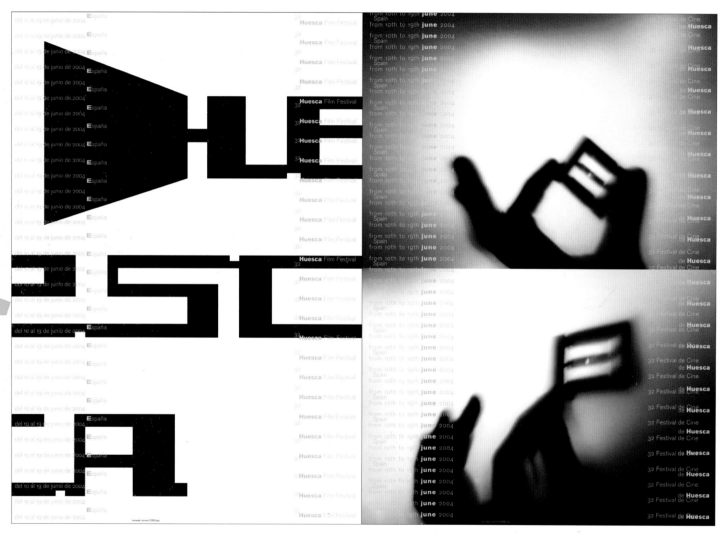

The pair of Huesca Film Festival posters (above) express the essence of film: one is typographic and one photographic. Both posters are further divided into two horizontal frames. In the typographic poster, Sonnoli shapes the word *Huesca* (the name of the small village that hosts the film festival) into a theater by outlining a space—perhaps a stage or screen—with the edges of the letterform and counterform. The word is repeated vertically but framed differently each time, to mimic the panning of a movie camera.

The photographic poster further reinforces cinematic ideas of movement, light, and shadow through a two-frame sequence of a letter *H* interacting with a hand. Both type and image are rendered in shadow, creating a direct visual relationship between them as they change poses from one frame to the next. Secondary text is positioned along the edge much like sprocket holes in strips of film.

Comune di Pesaro
Servizi Culturali

Circoscrizione
delle Colline e dei Castelli

Il lavoro delle donne
nei borghi rurali del pesarese

PESARO CULTURA

Comune di Pesaro
Biblioteca Centrale

Leggere negli anni
della Fenice e oltre
il mondo nuovo

4 lezioni di pedagogia della lettura
tenute dal professor Antonio Faeti
ordinario di Storia della Letteratura
per l'infanzia dell'Università di Bologna

Pesaro,
Palazzo Montani Antaldi, ore 16.30

01 | **24.03.1998**
In coffa d'albero
Sui modi di leggere,
sulle testimonianze
di lettori illustri,
sull'unicità della lettura,
sui rischi dei non lettori.

02 | **31.03.1998**
La biblioteca di Dylan Dog
La lettura oggi, collegamenti,
connessioni, rimandi, incroci,
nell'immaginario e con altri media.

03 | **07.04.1998**
I dodicenni amano Stephen King
I generi, le icone dell'orrore, le teste
vuote, l'eredità del feuilleton.

04 | **21.04.1998**
Un adolescente nel salotto
di Nonna Speranza
Sul significato ed il valore attuale
dei classici per l'infanzia,
sulla memoria perduta,
sul recupero di sedimenti comuni.

PESARO BIBLIOTECHE

PROJECT (LEFT)

Poster: *Il lavoro delle donne nei borghi rurali del pesarese* (The work of women in rural districts)

CLIENT

Comune di Pesaro
Servizi Culturali
Pesaro, Italy

Leonardo Sonnoli
CODEsign
Rimini, Italy

Type and image become one as the giant d (for *donne*, "women"), along with a tag announcing the date and time of the event, is "pinned" onto the poster for an event celebrating women's work.

PROJECT (RIGHT)

Poster: ABC reading pedagogy lectures

CLIENT

Comune di Pesaro
Biblioteca Centrale
Pesaro, Italy

Hand shadows mix with letterforms to reach the audience for a children's reading program at a library.

Comune di Pesaro
Biblioteca Centrale

Presentazione del libro
di Paolo Teobaldi
"La discarica"

interverrà Domenico Starnone
giornalista e scrittore
Sabato 7 novembre 1998,
ore 17.30
Sala del Consiglio comunale

PESARO BIBLIOTECHE

PROJECT (LEFT)

Poster for book presentation: *La discaria* (The Dump)

CLIENT

Comune di Pesaro
Biblioteca Centrale
Pesaro, Italy

The letterforms that spell *la discarica* ("the dump") become part of a seamless composition of type and image for a library program about Paolo Teobaldi's ironic novel of the same name.

PROJECT (RIGHT)

Poster: *AIDS tra utopia a realta: La centralita della persona* (AIDS between utopia and reality: The importance of the person)

CLIENT

Various sponsors

The man's head is integral to the letterform *A* from the word *AIDS*, in this poster promoting a conference on the role of men in the prevention of the disease.

III Convegno
Nazionale

AIDS tra utopia
e realtà
La centralità
della persona

·C.I.C.A. Coordinamento
Case Alloggio AIDS
Fondazione
Don Gaudiano
·CE.I.S. di Pesaro
Villa Moscati

In collaborazione con:
·Presidenza del Consiglio
Regionale delle Marche
·Provincia di Pesaro-Urbino
·Comune di Pesaro

Con il patrocinio di:
·Banca delle Marche

8, 9 maggio
Oasi S. Nicola, Pesaro
ad invito
10 maggio
Teatro Sperimentale, Pesaro
aperto al pubblico

Typography often exists in relation to paper—the printed page. Messages left behind on small scraps of paper have an intimacy that sparks human curiosity. We consider them chance information like fortunes in cookies, once concealed and now uncovered.

In both of these pieces, hidden meanings take the form of paper mementos. Their cryptic quality is enhanced by the fact that the individual letters remain disconnected, either on separate folded panels or on individual cardboard disks, strung together to make words. The tactile quality of the photographs emphasizes the sense of craft, of the human hand, in the forming of the messages. The impact of discovery is further amplified by the enlargement of the coded information within the large poster format.

INVERSION

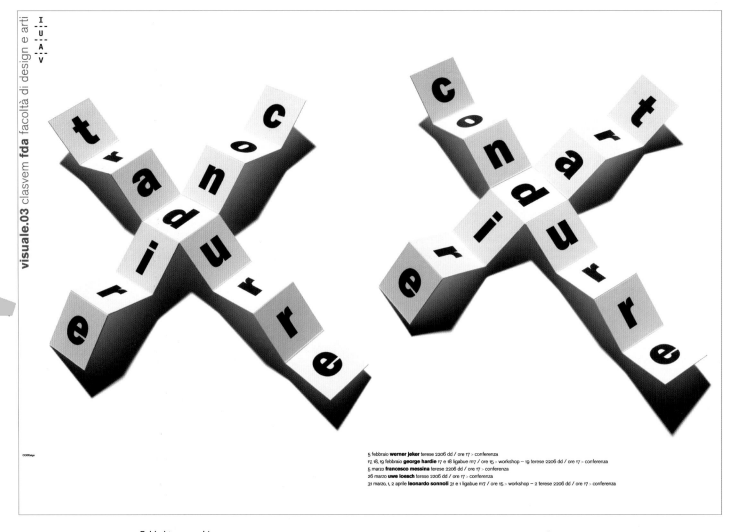

PROJECT
Poster: *Tradurre, Tradire, Condurre, Condire*
CLIENT
Università Iuav di Venezia, Architecture Venice, Italy
DESIGNER
Leonardo Sonnoli
CODEsign
Rimini, Italy

Folded typographic paper objects can be interpreted many ways in this poster by Leonardo Sonnoli for a series of design lectures.

Tradurre, tradire, condurre, condire (translate, betray, guide, flavor) is the message on Leonardo Sonnoli's poster for a series of lectures and workshops by five contemporary graphic designers: Werner Jeker, George Hardie, Francesco Messina, Uwe Loesch, and Sonnoli himself. The four verbs summarize the designers' varied approaches to translating messages and amplifying, meaning. Keeping in this spirit, Sonnoli has constructed cryptic crisscrossed intersections of words to further activate their meaning.

In discussing the concept for this poster advertising a dance performance, Michel Bouvet explained, "I wanted to use typography instead of any classical vision of dance." Hand-lettered placards appear like found objects bound onto a clothesline and span almost the entire width.

The clotheslines are reminiscent of ballet laces but have a contemporary edge. The designer further explains, "The string is used to represent the binding relationship between the choreographer's plan and the dancers' performance."

Letters strung together create a message reflecting the improvisational quality of a highly experimental dance company.

PROJECT
Poster: *Rendezvous chorégraphiques de Sceaux*
CLIENT
Les Gémeaux
Sceaux, France
DESIGNER
Michel Bouvet
Paris, France
PHOTOGRAPHER
Francis Laharrague
Fréjus, France

INVERSION

Monguzzi achieves a dramatic sense of space to express the dark and mysterious nature of Fausto Gerevini's photographs by constructing a complex yet direct gesture of the photographer's name winding through the picture plane.

Monguzzi's process for making the poster was very spontaneous. In his own words:

[For] this poster there are no sketches. I started immediately on my table playing with light; I was looking for the idea while manipulating a few elements. I wanted to build [Gerevini's] name photographically, using light, and I needed his name to become in some way enigmatic, like most of the photographs in the show. I printed the words Fausto Gerevini on film. The name was set on two lines without a precise idea, just as a trial.

I taped the negative film on a sheet of glass and laid the glass over four mineral water bottles sitting right under my drawing table lamp. Between the bottles I pushed a piece of thick white paper, a kind of tilted bridge, to get a bent projection surface for his name—I knew I needed curves to allude to his organic universe—and began to move the lamp and/or the paper. The results were quite deceiving. I therefore cut the front straight side of the paper on a generous curve and started moving the light and the inclination of the paper again. The miracle happened when the top part of the projected type reached the table. The idea was there! The piece of paper I had cut off, still slightly bent, was still on the table. I moved it carefully under the paper bridge to receive the accidental fragment of light (concave versus convex). Fausto came with his Sinar camera, he liked it, and we shot it.

PROJECT
**Poster for
Fausto Gerevini exhibition**
CLIENT
**Museo Cantonale d'Arte
Lugano, Switzerland**
DESIGNER
**Bruno Monguzzi
Meride, Switzerland**

The black wedge on the left contrasts with the curve and harmonizes with the letter A in the museum logo. The angled secondary type further reinforces the dramatic illusion of three-dimensional space.

In Bruno Monguzzi's book *A Designer's Perspective*, Italian designer and architect Pierluigi Cerri wrote a beautiful tribute to Monguzzi's talent as a designer: "He doesn't enclose his text in cages, but rather designs them, interprets them, makes them part of the visual process, manipulates them in rigorous dependence."

Radial letterforms activate this poster for a juried college art exhibition. The choice of type as the primary image is an insightful way of expressing the diversity of art forms in the show—ceramics, fibers, metals, painting, photography, printmaking, sculpture, and visual communication—without focusing too much on one particular discipline. The word *open* descends vertically and swings open like a door, breaking out of the picture plane to invite the viewer into the exhibition. The three-dimensional letterforms project shadows in reverse, like a staircase of light from a dark background into an illuminated foreground. Their multimedia presence and their upward movement also suggest learning and experimentation in the arts.

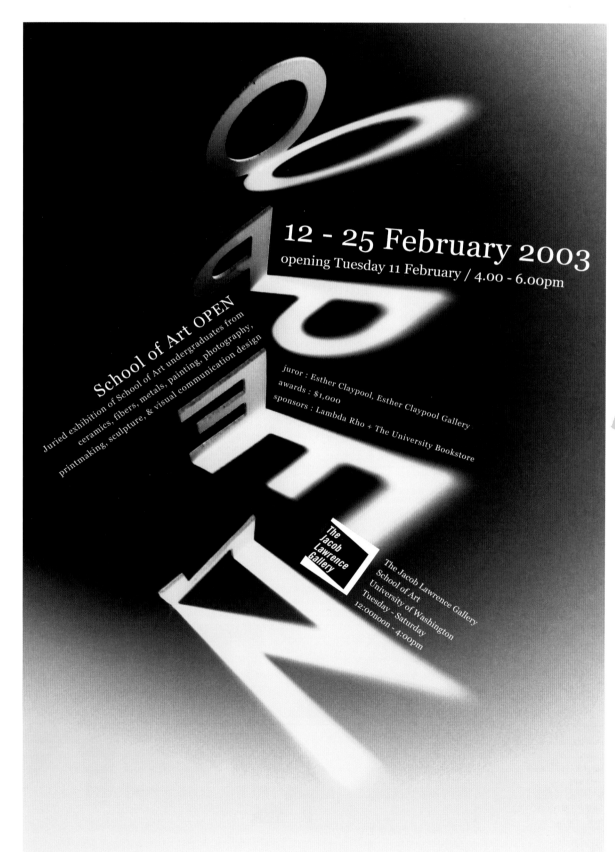

Winding words in space build momentum in these posters.

PROJECT
Poster: *School of Art*
OPEN
CLIENT
**School of Art, University of Washington
Seattle, USA**
DESIGNER
**Christopher Ozubko
Studio Ozubko
Seattle, USA**

INVERSION

Whimsical illustrations of
shoes are configured in
an abstract hierarchical
typographic arrangement
that interweaves soft
numerals, images, and
bands of text.

PROJECT
Posters for Musica Viva
CLIENT
Musica Viva Munich,
Germany
DESIGN
Günter Karl Bose
Berlin, Germany

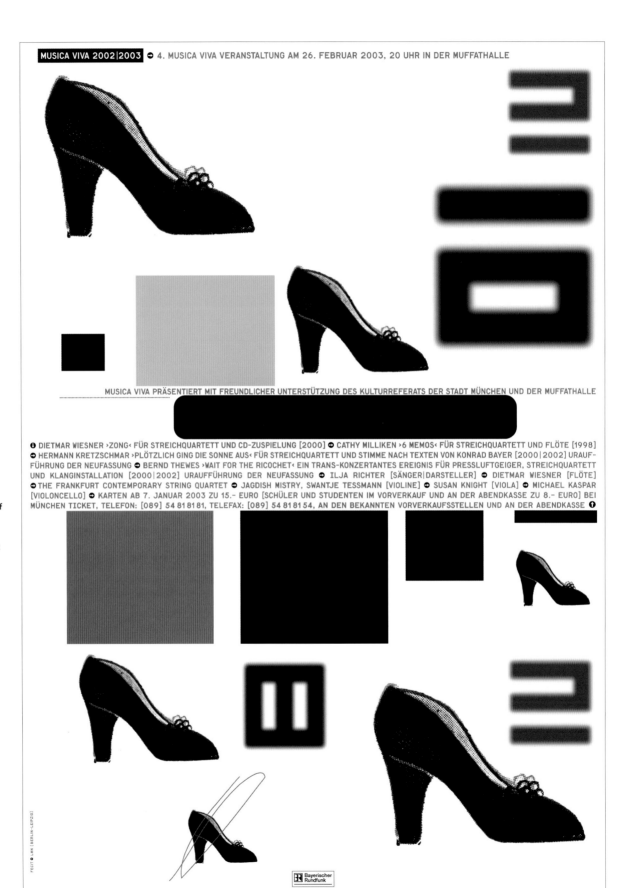

Applying numbers inspired
from late 1960s watches,
the designer Günter Karl
Bose has established a
clear identity for this
musical performance.

Musica Viva organizes concerts of late twentieth- and early twenty-first century avant-garde music. The organization introduces young composers and performers and also features established experimental musicians in each concert series.

For Berlin-based designer Günter Karl Bose, creating a series of monthly posters for the concerts presents interesting challenges. Graphic symbols—photographs, illustrations, or geometric forms—are used to represent each specific series.

Bose senses, however, that the graphic elements are not a direct translation of the music: "Music has its own language; graphic design is a separate language....I try not to duplicate the music, but represent it in the language of graphic design." With this in mind, he employs visual manifestations of rhythm, proportion, color, and form to visualize the essence of the musical performances.

In *Kieler Woche* (below left), submitted as an entry in an annual poster competition for a sailing event and summer festival on the Kiel Fjord in Germany, two-dimensional letters appear to skim across a full-bleed sapphire sea. A trail of backwash forms a V shape behind each character, making them resemble sailboats cutting through the surface of the water (poster.) The designer has executed this simple concept in perfect detail so that the illusion is never broken. There is an unanticipated shift in the viewer's perception as the eye and mind are both challenged to move back and forth between reading words and seeing pictures.

The letters appear animated in this poster for a lecture (below right) on movie and television typography. Multiple images of type fade and sharpen, re-creating the sense of motion in broadcast and title design. The type appears to bend as it moves across the surface of the poster; this illusion is further enhanced by the out-of-focus quality of the letters as they come off the surface.

PROJECT
Poster: *Kieler
Woche 2004*
CLIENT
Kieler Woche Poster
Design Competition
Kiel, Germany
DESIGNER/
PHOTOGRAPHER
Heribert Birnbach
Birnbach Design
Bonn, Germany

Words are deconstructed into letters, and letters become unfamiliar representations of familiar things (the sailboats) in this poster by Heribert Birnbach.

INVERSION

PROJECT
Poster for lecture by
Ralf Lobeck
CLIENT
University of Wuppertal
Wuppertal, Germany
DESIGNER/
PHOTOGRAPHER
Heribert Birnbach
Birnbach Design
Bonn, Germany

Letterforms materialize and dematerialize to show the unpredictable qualities of type in motion.

The information on this poster (below) takes the form of a plastic lettering template. Because the letters are punched out of plastic, the counterforms fall away and the letters lose all but their structural detail, making the viewer even more conscious of their geometry. The poster is announcing a seminar on design and business; the template is a ready-made object that acts as a metaphorical reminder that there are tried-and-true, routine practices for designers to appropriate from the seminar.

PROJECT
Poster for Lutz
Hackenberg Seminar
CLIENT
University of Wuppertal
Wuppertal, Germany
DESIGNER/
PHOTOGRAPHER
Heribert Birnbach
Birnbach Design
Bonn, Germany

In this poster for a seminar on design practices, a lettering template conveys all the necessary information.

VISUAL PUNS

This poster for an exhibition of Uwe Loesch's own work challenges the viewer with multiple interpretations. Loesch's unique approach to type and image was described very well by Dr. Jürgen Döring of the Museum für Kunst und Gewerbe in Hamburg: "The typographic elements in Uwe Loesch's posters merit special attention. The observer is required to think for himself, to operate with the categories of perception and truth....There is a frequent use of signs and symbols which are endowed with new significance by an unusual context."

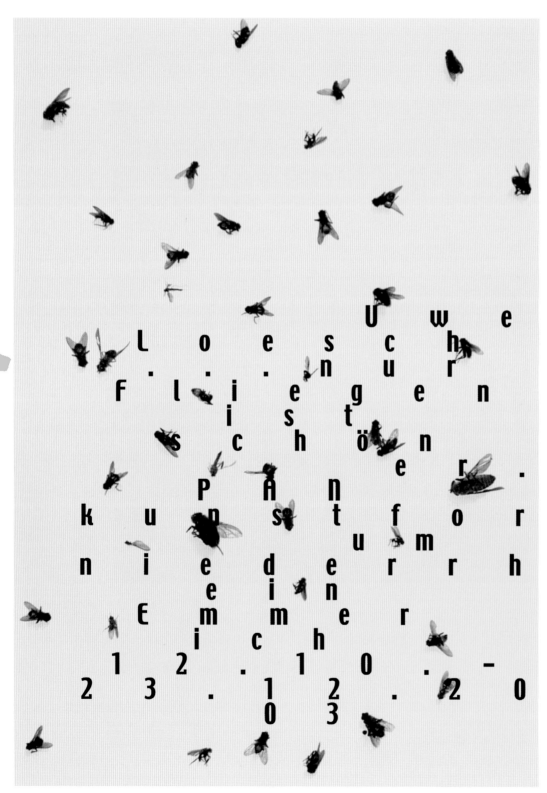

Uwe Loesch's poster for an exhibition of his own work contains a visual pun: does *fliegen* mean "flying" or "flies"?

PROJECT
Poster for exhibition: "...nur Fliegen ist schöner" (Only Flying Is More Beautiful)
CLIENT
Pan Kunstforum Niederrhein, Germany
DESIGNER
Uwe Loesch Erkrath, Germany

In German, the word *Fliegen* means not only "flying" but "flies." Loesch sets up a connection between the flies and the type by assigning them a uniform black color and distributing the type and the flies evenly across the surface. The resulting poster (opposite) poses more questions than it answers: Is he comparing designing to flying when he says only flying is more beautiful? Is he making fun of the concept of beauty by using a swarm of flies as the image? Is he joking that his work attracts flies? Anything is possible.

This billboard (below) was designed to expose the use of the Internet by neo Nazis to disseminate propaganda (*scheisse*, "shit"). The central image—a Hitler with shaved head and a "mustache" created by the letters *www*—is loaded with associations that visually connect the Internet to neo-fascist activity.

PROJECT
Billboard for the open-air exhibition *Irritations*
CLIENT
City of Mönchengladbach, Germany
DESIGNER
Uwe Loesch
Erkrath, Germany

Hitler's moustache is substituted with a website address in this billboard exposing the potential of the Internet to facilitate propaganda.

The typographic experimentation of the French graphic designer Robert Massin is personified in this poster for an exhibit of his work at the University of Quebec at Montreal. Stéphane Huot's portrait of Massin is a perfect depiction of his persona as a master of type and image. The flat large letterforms spell out his name—in Huot's words, "Type dances in his head like it dances in his work." The black and white silhouette is a reference to Massin's famous French book *La Cantatrice Chauve* (The Bald Soprano), an interpretation of the Eugene Ionesco play in which he placed high-contrast black and white figures and animated typography on the pages. Huot finishes his parody with a small inset photograph of a smiling mouth. Of his process designing this poster, Hout says, "This poster was done very quickly in one evening only. The process was very spontaneous and intuitive. I have designed it in a collage manner and I tried not to think too much to keep the playful aspect of it."

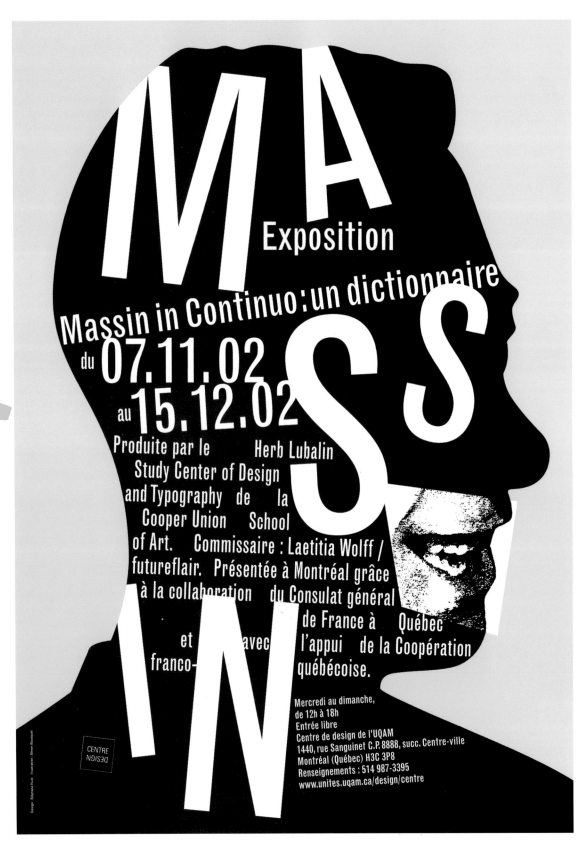

INVERSION

This poster, a portrait of Robert Massin for an exhibition of his work, uses scale change, rhythm, and alternating planar perspective to reflect his delight in telling typographic stories.

PROJECT
Poster for exposition:
"Massin in Continuo:
un dictionnaire"
CLIENT
Design Center, University of Quebec in Montreal (l'UQAM)
DESIGNER
Stéphane Huot
Montreal, Quebec

This poster for a retrospective of Paul Newman's films is a typographic characterization of the actor: the letters of his name act as framing devices for his portrait. The designer, Ralph Schraivogel, has chosen a condensed typeface and has positioned the type vertically in strips across the page, delivering the image as a series of consecutive frames, as in a film. The beautiful composition of the letterforms places the actor's features at an angle in harmony with the shaped windows and breaks his name into two syllables that share letters and read in both directions to fashion an alluring mask. The fact that Schraivogel was able to create such a cohesive portrait of Paul Newman with a such a simple photograph reveals his mastery of typography and composition. Remarkably humble, he says of this poster, " I never try to make a poster that looks like a poster. But if one does in spite of all, I guess it is a good one."

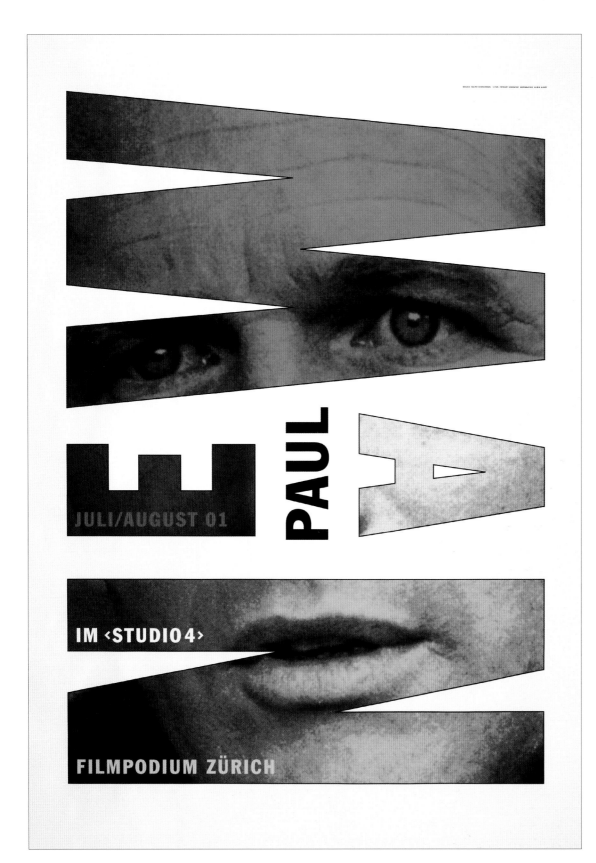

The assorted colors suggest the multiplicity of Paul Newman's characters; it is probably no coincidence that the eyes fall in the blue area.

PROJECT
Poster: *Paul Newman*
CLIENT
FilmPodium Zürich
Zurich, Switzerland
DESIGNER
Ralph Schraivogel
Atelier Schraivogel
Zurich, Switzerland

Even though the poster is printed with simple flat areas of color, the light-colored text/barges in the foreground create a tremendous sense of depth as they contrast with the darker, more subdued values used in the text/barges in the background.

PROJECT
Poster: *Bateaux sur l'eau, rivières, et canaux* (Barges on water, rivers, and canals)

CLIENT
Armada Rouen
Rouen, France

DESIGN
Philippe Apeloig
Apeloig Design
Paris, France

Philippe Apeloig makes type into image in a unique solution for a poster (opposite) promoting an exhibition of small barge models on a river in Rouen, France. Rather than rely on a conventional photographic approach, Apeloig has elected to illustrate the barges with letterforms. Suspended in a blue field, the essential text transforms itself from the function of information into the illusion of barges floating on the water's surface. The effect is further supported by that same information inverted, in reflective form, positioned under each word. The use of horizontal partially obscured text, in contrast to the verticality of the poster format, entices the viewer with only a limited exposure.

In these posters (above) for the year of Brazil in France, letterforms create an atmosphere rather than construct a picture. Form, counterform, and color set up a lively vibration between figure and ground. Clusters of letters interact to mimic the rhythm of Brazilian culture.

PROJECT
Poster: *Brésil, Brésils: Année du Brésil en France* (Brazil, Brazils: The Year of Brazil in France)
CLIENT
Self
DESIGN
Philippe Apeloig
Apeloig Design
Paris, France

This large-format typographic poster was silk-screened in two versions to further explore multiple interactions of color.

Niklaus Troxler's *Typo Plakate* poster proves that type alone can create a distinct image. Here, the viewer is immediately caught off guard by the large white rectangle in the middle of the poster: this strong representation of poster space is established instantaneously and efficiently. However, the designer achieves this effect of monumental simplicity through many subtle details of placement, color, and scale. These typographic nuances are the building blocks of both the image and the message of "the typographic poster."

The essence of the poster—its economy, directness, and simplicity—is built into the form of these two posters for poster exhibitions. Manifestations and gestures intrinsic to the poster are employed include framing, folding, posting, and large-scale typography.

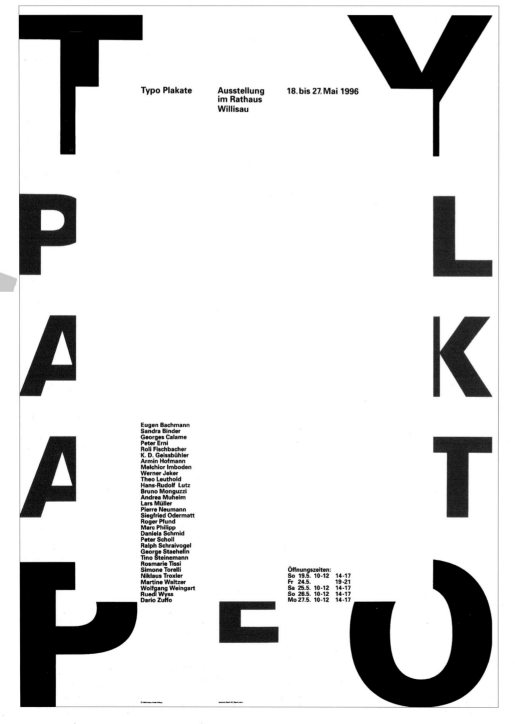

INVERSION

The large white rectangle almost obliterates the words *Typo Plakate*, but reinforces the image of a poster. Smaller blocks of text delineate the edge of the rectangle and complete the illusion.

PROJECT
**Poster: *Typo Plakate*
(Typographic Posters)**
CLIENT
**Ausstellung im Rathaus
Willisau, Switzerland**
DESIGNER
**Niklaus Troxler
Niklaus Troxler
Graphic Design
Willisau, Switzerland**

In Philippe Apeloig's poster, each letter manifests itself as its own individual poster to make a "wall" of smaller posters. This simultaneously expresses the grouping systems that are inherent in both the alphabet and in the poster. A sequence of evenly spaced rectangles, each containing one capital letter—extra-bold and white on a bright colored field—sets up a fascinating device to reveal the message. The letterforms are defined by white space in combination with lines of black text. The deciphering of each letter not only announces the show but illustrates the capacity of the poster to embody communication.

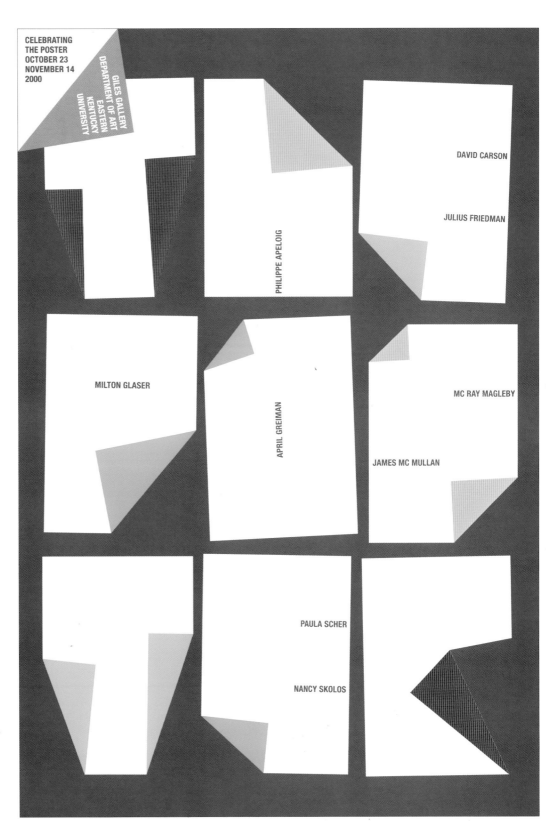

The designer uses type as image to epitomize the poster as a concrete system of communication.

PROJECT
Poster: *Celebrating the Poster*
CLIENT
**Eastern Kentucky University
Richmond, Kentucky, USA**
DESIGNER
**Philippe Apeloig
Apeloig Design
Paris, France**

Minoru Niijima has an exceptional ability to tease out the essential qualities of an idea and express it with pure typography. "Through a simple forming operation, we remove meaning from words and turn them into decoration," he says of the design process.

Niijima has found a voice through typography—a middle ground between the form and symbolic meaning of letters. His designs go beyond the obvious, and their elegance is a result of taking a simple concept and finessing the details to perfection. This is evident in his poster (below)

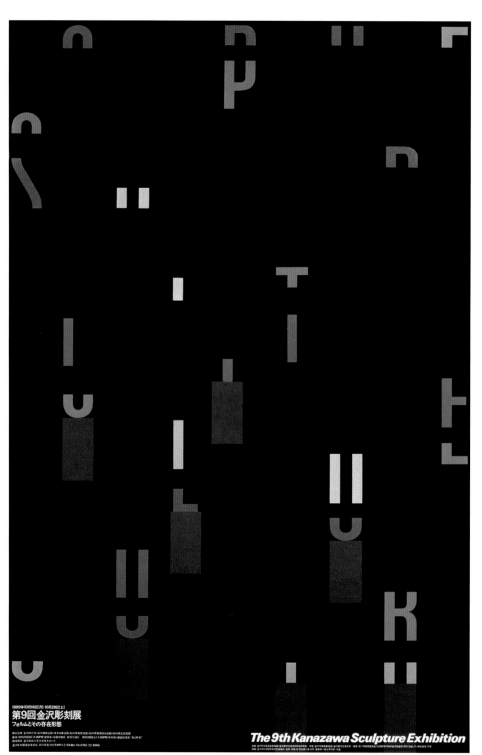

Many of the letterforms are highlighted with light colors, making them appear as if they are under the spotlight in an expansive dark space.

PROJECT
Poster for 9th Kanazawa Sculpture Exhibition
CLIENT
Kanazawa Sculpture Exhibition Committee
DESIGNER
Minoru Niijima Tokyo, Japan

for a sculpture exhibition Here, the abstraction of letters into sculpture is immediately clear and amusing. Rectangles act as pedestals supporting fragments of letters to present both a pictorial and objective text reading.

The illusion of a gallery space is subliminally heightened by the placement of the letter-objects in the picture plane against the perimeter of the poster; it's as if they were pushed up against an exhibition wall.

Niijima's poster promoting Emerging Japanese Architects (below) is another striking example of type as image. Here he has turned words sideways to shape a skyscraper against a black night sky. The extremely condensed letterforms stack up to build the facade of a multistory high-rise building. Again color values are manipulated to create an atmosphere of reality within the fiction of this typographic scenario. The viewer can see evidence of activity in the selectively lit stories of the building.

This typographic configuration pushes the limits of legibility as it reinforces the theme of emergence and recognition.

PROJECT
Poster: *Emerging Japanese Architects of the 1990s*
CLIENT
E.J.A. Committee
DESIGNER
Minoru Niijima
Tokyo, Japan

The concept behind this poster is simple: type as DNA. The execution, however, is impeccable—a composition, a string of letters that fills the space with an elegance equal to the notion of the magic of DNA. The words *life science design award / concepts for a better life* are placed on two lines on a slight diagonal across the frame to reinforce the state of flux and activate the illusion of the double helix. Both strands of type are rendered in perspective, but the white type is anchored to the picture plane (because the eye connects the white color to the paper color) while the shadowed type breathes in and out of the surface, representing an ethereal substance that has been discovered but not fully comprehended.

The title of this poster builds an ethereal strand of DNA that is set off against a black background to suggest the intangible realm of science.

PROJECT
Poster announcing Life Science Design Award
CLIENT
Design Center North Rhine Westphalia Essen, Germany
DESIGNER
Uwe Loesch Erkrath, Germany

This poster is the opposite of scientific, but like Loesch's DNA poster at left, it is a typographic snapshot of something intangible, in this case the artist/designer Ed Fella's way of thinking and seeing. His name, rendered with his signature hand-drawn lettering, moves effortlessly from tightly outlined block letters to charcoal-drawn loops and back. This configuration is mirrored so that his first name is legible in one direction and his last name in the other. The backwards *Ed* also reveals an intentional or perhaps an unintentional secondary message: 3D. This is a fitting subtext because Fella's designs often engineer a very complex sense of space.

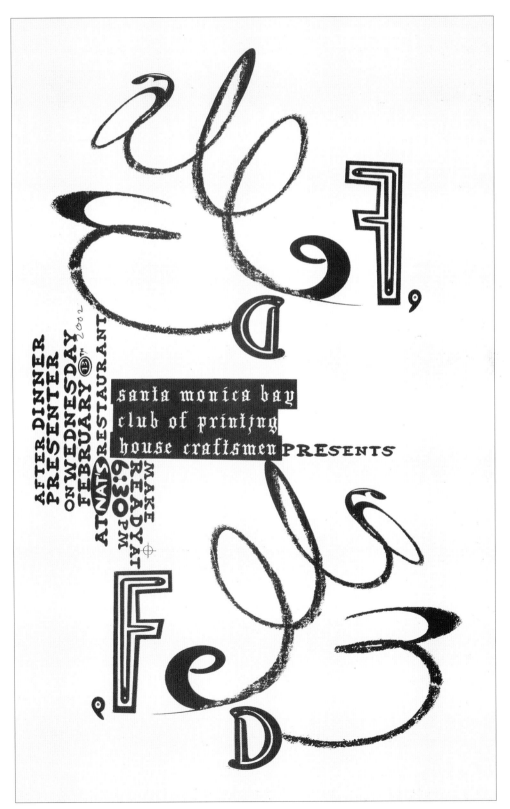

The reversal of the names in this poster for a lecture at a club of printers relates to the way printing works; the plate is reversed and the reproduction is positive.

PROJECT
**Flier for presentation
by Ed Fella**
CLIENT
**Santa Monica Bay Club of
Printing House Craftsmen
Santa Monica, California,
USA**
DESIGN
**Ed Fella
Valencia, California, USA**

Swiss designer Niklaus Troxler's avid interest and love of jazz music is illustrated quite vividly in his *Jazz in Willisau* posters. In these pieces, Troxler makes the invisible world of music visible. For example, vibrating text and repeated letterforms of varying intensities strongly suggest improvisational jazz rhythms in the poster (below right) for a performance of the Carlo Actis Dato Quartet. Each word is charged with a strong sense of energy, which captures the frenetic pacing and descending repetitions of the quartet's live performances.

PROJECT
Poster for Ellery Eskelin
and Han Bennick
CLIENT
Jazz in Willisau
Willisau, Switzerland
DESIGNER
Niklaus Troxler
Niklaus Troxler
Graphic Design
Willisau, Switzerland

Troxler's poster for the performance of a saxophone and drum jazz duo uses splattered ink to suggest bursts of sound and improvisations.

PROJECT
Poster for Carlo
Actis Dato Quartet
CLIENT
Jazz in Willisau
Willisau, Switzerland
DESIGNER
Niklaus Troxler
Niklaus Troxler
Graphic Design
Willisau, Switzerland

The use of black and white focuses attention on the subtle details and irregularities in the structure of the typography, pushing the limits of legibility.

One of a series of biannual posters for African films, this composition incorporates the reverberating rhythms that reflect the culture at the heart of the Cinémafrica festival.

The letters operate as individual forces, rendered in multiple frames and comprehended—many per second—to capture the energy of film. This poster also illustrates aspects of fragmentation, as the letters gain momentum from the optical pulse of the background.

In this poster for Cinémafrica, Ralph Schraivogel animates letterforms to interpret cinematic time and space.

PROJECT
Poster for film festival
CLIENT
**Afrika-Filmtage/
Filmpodium
Zurich, Switzerland**
DESIGNER
**Ralph Schraivogel
Atelier Schraivogel
Zurich, Switzerland**

PROJECT
Millennium poster
CLIENT
**New Millennium
Experience Company
(NMEC)
London, UK**
DESIGNER
**Siobhan Keaney
London, UK**

This computer-generated
composition is made up
of every date in the past
2000 years.

INVERSION

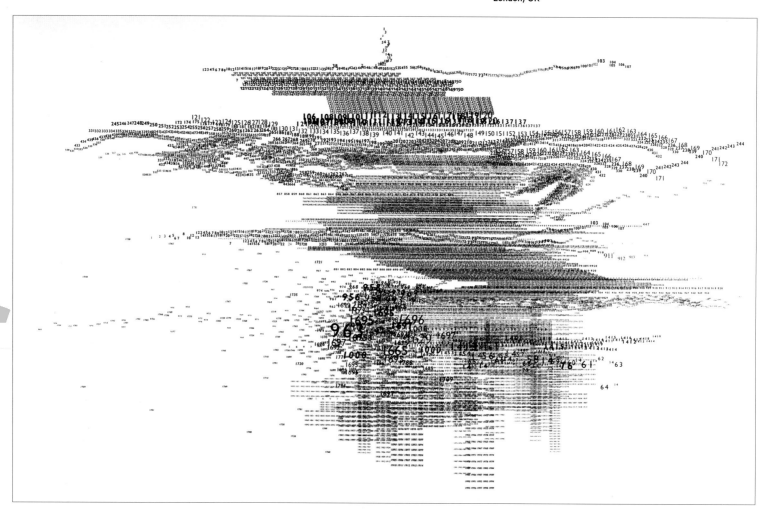

This large-format poster contains every date from the last two millennia. As Siobhan Keaney describes, "I worked on this poster over a number of days….I set about filling the space with the dates…and the structure emerged naturally." The piece takes on the presence of a monumental doodle. As in most of Keaney's work, the feeling is quite organic; it is easy to imagine her starting in one place on the page and letting the process unfold much like a painting. Because of its expanse and fluidity, it is quite remarkable that this piece was designed on a computer. Its cloudlike formation, concentrated in areas and dissipated in others, has a gentle quality and lighthandedness that makes Keaney's work unique.

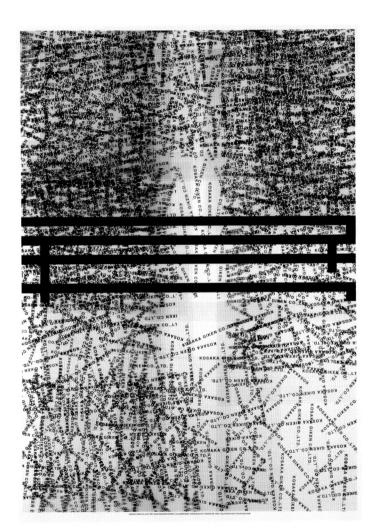

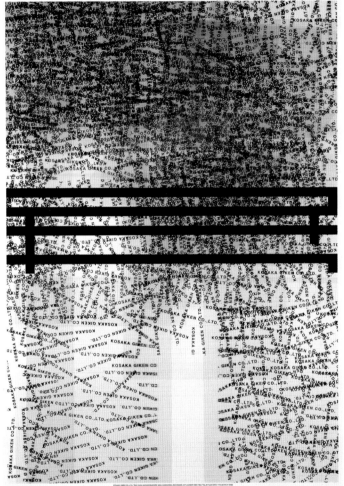

PROJECT
Poster for building
consultancy
CLIENT
Kosaka-Giken
DESIGNER
Yasuhiro Sawada
Yasuhiro Sawada
Design Studio
Tokyo, Japan

The multiple pieces of
type appear to be sorted
as they pass through the
poster space, suggesting
the many solutions that
the company generates.

Kosaka Giken is a construction company whose activity covers a wide
range of areas including design, surveying, environmental research,
and the development of building materials. The Japanese katakana
character has been stretched across the poster to symbolize the breadth
of the company's activities; it spells out the company's name, *KoSaKa*.
The repetition of the words *Kosaka Giken Co. Ltd.* in smaller type builds
up density, representing the many construction possibilities and ideas
that the company can address.

This poster resembles a slot machine, with three white fields framing aligned rows of menu bars and bulleted messages about integrated computer technology and Internet commerce. Two-thirds of the way down on the page, the viewer sees a densely layered pile of barely legible snippets of Malcolm McLaren's philosophy, commentary, and list of milestones in his musical career. The overall effect is that of an absurd collection of artifacts.

Poster for a touring exhibition titled "Casino of Authenticity and Karaoke," an installation looking at the life and art of Malcolm McLaren— artist, fashion designer, and manager of such punk rock bands as the Sex Pistols in the late 1970s.

PROJECT
Poster for Malcolm McLaren's "Casino of Authenticity and Karaoke" exhibition
CLIENT
Malcolm McLaren London, UK
DESIGNER
Why Not Associates London, UK

PROJECT
Poster: *Sportdesign*
CLIENT
**Museum für Gestaltung
Zurich, Switzerland**
DESIGNER
**Martin Woodtli
Zurich, Switzerland**

Fashioned between the counterforms of the S are colorful op art diagrams from soccer, hockey, and other sports, as well as graphic checkers and dots.

This poster, designed for an exhibit on sport design at the Museum für Gestaltung, is an example of Martin Woodtli's skill at merging form, function, style, and engineering. The viewer's interaction with this poster is much like playing a game. The word *sports* in the foreground has a meshlike quality that positions the viewer, like an opponent, on the other side of a net. Beyond the screen of type, the viewer is drawn in by the lively colors and patterns that make up the world of sports and gaming. The large letter *S* has multiple associations: a varsity letter, racetrack, or even a dollar sign. The overall poster takes on the configuration of a stadium, with the type actively involved in expressing the message.

THOUGHT AS IMAGE

This project was done as a public service announcement for Radio Scotland with the tag line *Rediscover the power of the spoken word.* Jonathan Barnbrook was asked to animate sound bites from the radio broadcast, and he used his elegant typefaces to express the "spirituality" of the words.

The voiceover is beautifully timed in rhythm to the melodic speech of the man delivering the message, *"These are the things that life is made of..."*

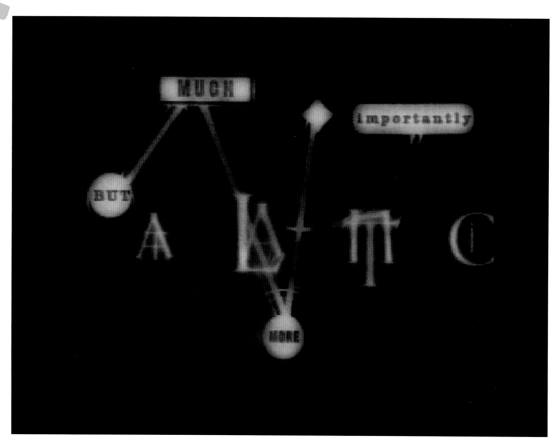

"...I wanted to see what the Atlantic was like... can only see it by going... but much more importantly I wanted to see what I was like on the Atlantic."

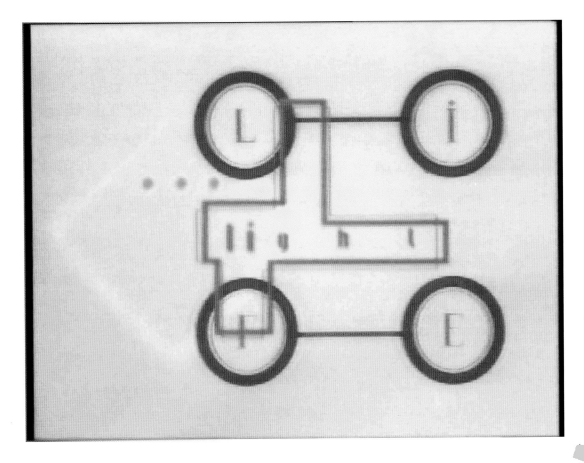

The voice continues: *"What's wrong with romance? It brings light in to life...into your own life, and into other people's lives. God forbid that we were all practical pragmatists."*

PROJECT
Web Animation
"True Romance"
CLIENT
BBC Radio Scotland
Glasgow, Scotland
DESIGNER
Jonathan Barnbrook
Barnbrook Design
London, UK
ADVERTISING AGENCY
Faulds Advertising
Edinburgh, Scotland

In the hands of designer Catherine Zask, typography is molded into animated thoughts that speak from the page. This series of posters occupies a position just at the edge of the type/image spectrum, where typography's informative and expressive boundaries become blurred.

INVERSION

Lines connecting the typographic elements are animated like a conductor's baton and direct the reading of this poster promoting a performance event.

PROJECT
Poster: *Saison 2003–2004/L'Hippodrome, en travaux*
CLIENT
L'Hippodrome, scène nationale de Douai
Douai, France
DESIGNER
Catherine Zask
Paris, France

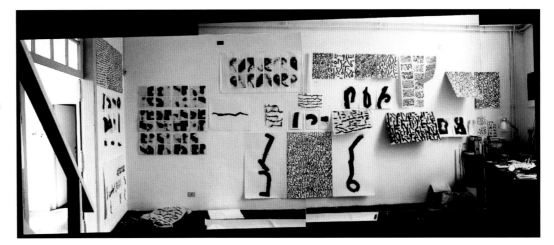

Catherine Zask's
Rome studio

From "the beats of letter strokes" the designer distilled her own font, Alfabetempo, which she used for an invitation (below right) to a solo exhibition of her work at the Galerie Anatome in Paris.

A further investigation into the imaginative use of text is evident in the two posters for L'Hippodrome in Douai, France. The first (below left) was intended as an introduction to the 2003–2004 season of events at the theater complex. Here, the designer modified the characters in the dates and the location in order to create an architectural space to frame the names of the composers, performers, and authors of upcoming performances.

For a performance by the hip-hop group Douar, the individual letterforms of the group's name were manipulated to mimic the movements of the performers on stage. The secondary text was then projected forward, at different angles, suggesting the rhythms of their music.

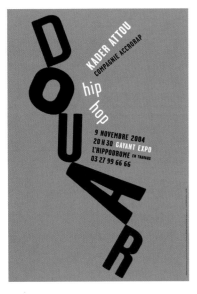

PROJECT
Poster promoting hip-hop performance by Douar
CLIENT
L'Hippodrome, scène nationale de Douai Douai, France
DESIGNER
Catherine Zask Paris, France

This use of highly stylized compositional text, suggesting emotions expressed in a musical performance, illustrates the effectiveness of type as image.

PROJECT
Invitation card and poster for Catherine Zask exhibition
CLIENT
Galerie Anatome Paris, France
DESIGNER
Catherine Zask Paris, France

The simplicity of the designer's name cascading down on a black background is a clear representation of both Zask's design style and the vitality of her personal typographic investigations.

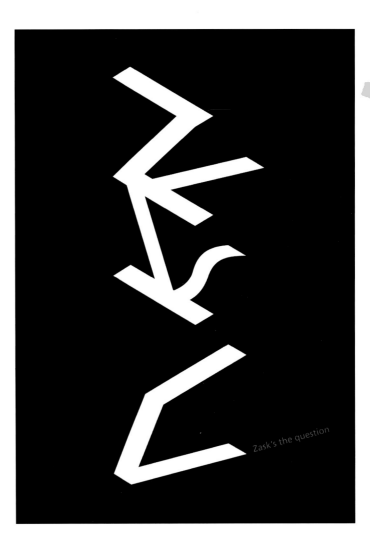

Nancy Skolos and
Thomas Wedell
Skolos-Wedell
125 Green Street
Canton, MA 02021
USA
www.skolos-wedell.com
*70, 71, 106, 107, 110, 132-135,
150-153*

Leonardo Sonnoli
CODEsign
via Giordano Bruno 51
Rimini 47900
Italy
120, 156-160

David Tartakover
Tartakover Design
34 Chelouche Street
Tel Aviv 65149
Israel
13, 104, 105, 110

Lucille Tenazas
Tenazas Design
1401 Shotwell Street
San Francisco, CA 94110
USA
www.tenazasdesign.com
52, 53

Niklaus Troxler
Niklaus Troxler Graphic Design
Bahnhofstrasse 22
Postfach
6130 Willisau
Switzerland
www.troxlerart.ch
174, 180

Martin Woodtli
Schoeneggstrasse 5
CH-8004 Zurich
Switzerland
www.woodt.li
136, 137, 144, 145, 185

Catherine Zask
220 rue du Faubourg-
Saint-Martin
75010 Paris
France
www.catherinezask.com
188, 189

BIBLIOGRAPHY

Aldersey-Williams, Hugh; Lorraine Wild; Daralice Boles; Katherine & Michael McCoy; Roy Slade; Niels Diffrient. *The New Cranbrook Design Discourse.* New York: Rizzoli International Publications, 1990.

Barthes, Roland. *The Photographic Message: A Barthes Reader,* edited by Susan Sontag. New York: The Noonday Press, 1991.

Bayer, Johnathan. *Reading Photographs: Understanding the Aesthetics of Photography.* New York: Random House, 1977.

Blossfeldt, Karl. *Urformen der Kunst Wundergarten der Natur: das Fotografische Werk in Einem Band.* Munich: Schirmer-Mosel, 1994.

Cato, Ken, ed. *First Choice: Leading International Designers Select the Very Best of Their Own Work.* Victoria, Australia: The Images Publishing Group, 2003.

Elam, Kimberly. *Expressive Typography: The Word as Image.* New York: Van Nostrand Reinhold, 1990.

14th Festival International de L'affiche et des Arts Graphiques. *Chamont 03.* Chaumont: Collection Dutailly, 2003.

He, Jianping, ed. *Bruno Monguzzi.* Guangdong, China: Lingnan Art Publishing House, 2004.

He, Jianping, ed. *David Tartakover.* Chongqing, China: Chongqing Publishing House, 2005.

Kolunen, Veijo, and Kari Savolainen, ed. *Lahti Poster Biennial 2005: The 15th International Poster Biennial.* Lahti, Finland: Grafia, 2005.

Korea Institute of Design Promotion (KIDP). *The 2nd Korea International Poster Biennale.* Seongnam City: Korea Institute of Design Promotion, 2004.

Kunz, Willi. *Typography: Macro- and Microaesthetics: Fundamentals of Typographic Design,* 2nd rev. ed. Zurich: Verlag Niggli, 2000.

Loesch, Uwe, and Students. *Master & Students.* Beijing: China Youth Press, 2004.

Lyons, Nathan, ed. *Photographers on Photography.* Englewood Cliffs, N.J.: Prentice-Hall, 1966.

Marzona, Egidio, ed. *Bauhaus Photography.* Cambridge, Mass.: The MIT Press, 1985.

McLuhan, Marshall. *Understanding Media: The Extensions of Man.* Cambridge, Mass.: The MIT Press, 1964.

Meggs, Philip B. *Type & Image: The Language of Graphic Design.* New York: Van Nostrand Reinhold, 1992.

Museum für Gestaltung Zürich. *Poster Collection: Posters for Exhibitions 1980–2000.* Zurich: Museum für Gestaltung Zürich & Lars Müller Publishers, 2001.

Museum für Kunst und Gewerbe Hamburg. *Uwe Loesch Nichtsdestoweniger Plakate.* Mainz, Germany: Verlag Hermann Schmidt, 1997.

Museum of Modern Art, Toyama. *The 6th International Poster Triennial in Toyama 2000 Catalog.* Toyama, Japan: The Museum of Modern Art, Toyama, 2000.

Nunoo-Quarcoo, Franc. *Bruno Monguzzi: A Designer's Perspective.* Baltimore: The Fine Arts Gallery, University of Maryland, 1998.

Poster Museum at Wilanów. *19th International Poster Biennale.* Warsaw, Poland, 2004.

Poynor, Rick. *No More Rules: Graphic Design and Postmodernism.* New Haven, Conn.: Yale University Press, 2003.

Rand, Paul. "Thoughts on the Poster: Lecture delivered in connection with the inaugural exhibition of the Swiss Institute, featuring posters by Armin Hofmann." New York, May 8, 1986. www.thegalleriesatmoore.org/publications/baselah.shtml

Samara, Timothy. *Making and Breaking the Grid: A Graphic Design Layout Workshop.* Gloucester, Mass.: Rockport Publishers, 2002.

Schraivogel, Ralph. *Poster Collection.* Zürich: Zürcher Fachhochschule & Lars Müller Publishers, 2003.

Sontag, Susan. *A Barthes Reader in Einem Band.* Munich: Schirmer-Mosel, 1994.

Teitelbaum, Matthew, ed. *Montage And Modern Life: 1919–1942.* Cambridge, Mass.: The MIT Press, 1992.

Troxler, Niklaus, and Lars Müller. *Jazz Blvd.: Niklaus Troxler Posters.* Baden, Switzerland: Lars Müller Publishers, 1999.

ACKNOWLEDGMENTS

First and foremost, we acknowledge with heartfelt thanks the luminous designers who made this publication possible. We are grateful not only for their generosity in sharing their extraordinary work and inspirational ideas, but even more thankful to them for creating the work in the first place.

Thank you to Kristin Ellison, Rockport's acquisitions editor, who invited us to do this project; and to Penny Stratton, copy editor; Rochelle Bourgault, project manager; and Regina Grenier, design project manager.

We are also indebted to our colleagues at the Rhode Island School of Design who have been our mentors and friends; and are very appreciative of a Faculty Professional Development Grant that supported our travel to Berlin to interview many of the designers.

A special thank you to our neighbors John and Tina Malouf, for forcing us to leave the studio every so often, and also to our friends Alison Angel and Donald Russell for encouragement, editing, and entertainment along the way.

ABOUT THE AUTHORS

Nancy Skolos and Thomas Wedell
Principals in Skolos-Wedell, an interdisciplinary design and photography studio

Husband and wife, the two work to diminish the boundaries between graphic design and photography—creating collaged three-dimensional images influenced by modern painting, technology, and architecture. With a home/studio halfway between Boston and Providence, they balance their commitments to professional practice and teaching at the Rhode Island School of Design.

The studio's work has received numerous awards and has been widely published and exhibited. Skolos-Wedell's posters are included in the graphic design collections of the Museum of Modern Art, the Metropolitan Museum of Art, the Library of Congress, the Israel Museum (Jerusalem), the Museum für Gestaltung (Zurich), and the Bibliothèque Nationale de France. Skolos is an elected member of the Alliance Graphique Internationale.

www.skolos-wedell.com

BOOK AND COVER DESIGN
Nancy Skolos, Thomas Wedell
Skolos-Wedell
PRODUCTION ASSISTANCE
Asya Palatova, Leanna Harada
TYPEFACE DESIGN
Cyrus Highsmith
TYPEFACES
Prensa and Relay
The Font Bureau, Inc.
CERAMIC DISPLAY LETTERS
Frank J. Mitten Company
(The letters were found at a
yard sale in Erie, Pennsylvania
by Kenneth R. Krayer Jr.)